187 Things You Should Know

about

The War of 1812

T0355437

187 Things You Should Know about the War of 1812

DONALD R. HICKEY

BALTIMORE
MARYLAND HISTORICAL SOCIETY
2012

Maryland Historical Society
201 W. Monument Street
Baltimore, Maryland, 21201
www.mdhs.org

Library of Congress Cataloging-in-Publication Data

Hickey, Donald R., 1944-
187 things you should know about the War of 1812 / Donald R.
Hickey.
    p. cm.
    Causes and Character -- The First Invasion of Canada -- The
Second Invasion of Canada -- The British Counterstrike -- The
End of the War -- The Legacy --Chronology -- Further Reading.
    Includes bibliographical references and index.
    ISBN 978-0-9842135-2-8 (alk. paper)
    1. United States--History--War of 1812. I. Title.
    E354.H54 2012
    973.5'2--dc23
                                            2012006937

Manufactured in the United States of America. The paper used in
this publication meets the minimum requirements of the American
National Standard for Information Sciences Permanence of Paper for
Printed Library Materials ANSI Z39.48-1984.

Frontispiece: The U.S. Frigate *Constitution* and the British frigate
Guerrière. (Engraving by Alonzo Chappel. Library of Congress.)

Contents

—◆◆◆◆—

Introduction

More than twenty years ago, I wrote a book on the War of 1812 with the subtitle "A Forgotten Conflict." It seemed to me that our second war with Great Britain was largely forgotten, overshadowed by the Revolution and the Civil War, those monumental conflicts that framed this momentous period in American history, and that the public knew little about the War of 1812. Scholars were still debating the causes and consequences of the conflict, and they could not even agree on who, if anyone, had actually won. Given this uncertainty, it is little wonder that most people, even those who were well educated, had little understanding of the war.

In Great Britain, the war was all but forgotten. Indeed, the very term "War of 1812" was most likely to conjure up images of Napoleon's massive invasion of Russia. If the American war was remembered at all, it was dismissed as an insignificant footnote to the much grander and more consequential Napoleonic Wars. In the United States, all that survived in the public memory were a couple of sayings—"Don't give up the ship" and "We have met the enemy and they are ours"—and a few of the war's highlights that reflected well on the young republic— the writing of "The Star-Spangled Banner," the naval laurels earned by "Old Ironsides," and Andrew Jackson's spectacular victory at New Orleans. In Canada, the war loomed much larger because it was the closest thing that people there had to a revolution or a civil war. Yet even in Canada people mainly remembered how a few high-profile heroes—Major General Isaac Brock, the Shawnee leader Tecumseh, and Laura Secord—had worked together to beat back the American invaders. Beyond this, the war there, as elsewhere, was terra incognita.

Although a great many books and articles on the war have appeared in the last twenty years, public perceptions have not changed much. The war is still a largely forgotten conflict.

Students of the war hope this will change with the Bicentennial. The two hundredth anniversaries of the key events—from the run-up to the war in 1811–12 to its conclusion in 1815—are being commemorated with festivals and re-enactments; with conferences, books, and articles; with proclamations and speeches; and, of course, with all sorts of memorabilia. In spite of all the hoopla, however, many people may still feel that they lack a clear understanding of what the War of 1812 was all about.

The purpose of this book is to fill that gap by providing a short introduction to the war. Rather than writing a conventional narrative, I have presented the pertinent information by answering a series of questions. My hope is that this format will make the material easy to digest and yet still provide the reader all the relevant information needed to understand the War of 1812 and, in turn, to appreciate each phase of the Bicentennial.

⟶◆⟵

For reading all or part of an earlier draft of the manuscript and making helpful suggestions, I would like to thank Connie D. Clark, Kathryn Roberts Morrow, Charles Berthold, and Frank Pytko. I also had help from fellow students of the war. Donald E. Graves and John Grodzinski read portions of the manuscript and answered my questions on the war's military history and the Canadian side of the story, and Christine Hughes supplied valuable information on the war at sea. I profited from other suggestions made by Gene Brissie, and I am indebted to Tracy Ellen Smith for the maps. As always, I owe a special debt to the staff at the U.S. Conn Library at Wayne State College. Dave Graber, Charissa

Loftis, Bill Van Arsdale, and Mary Woehler ran down information or sources for me, and Terri Headley continued her superb work at the interlibrary loan desk.

Don Hickey
Wayne State College
March 1, 2012
dohicke1@wsc.edu

CHAPTER ONE

Causes and Character

1 | Who fought in the War of 1812?

The principal antagonists were the United States and Great Britain. Because the United States targeted Britain's North American provinces, British subjects living in what is now the Dominion of Canada were also involved. In addition, both sides had Indian allies.

2 | How long did the war last?

Officially, for thirty-four months. The conflict began on June 18, 1812, when the United States declared war. The British learned of the declaration of war on July 30 but, hoping that peace might be restored, did not authorize reprisals until October 13. The war officially ended on February 16, 1815, when both sides ordered a suspension of hostilities following the ratification of the peace treaty. Because communication across the Atlantic was slow, there were minor military engagements in remote theaters for several months thereafter, and the United States did not make peace with the last Indian tribes until June 1816.

3 | Who were the American war leaders?

The American war effort was directed by President James Madison, who had assumed office in 1809. He was assisted by James

James Madison (1751–1836) was president during the War of 1812. Shy and scholarly, he was probably better cast to be a college professor than the wartime commander-in-chief in this tumultuous period. (J. A. Spencer, History of the United States.*)*

Monroe, who served as secretary of state and then as secretary of war; John Armstrong, who preceded Monroe as secretary of war; Albert Gallatin, the secretary of the treasury; and William Jones, who served for a time as secretary of the navy. Congress also had considerable input because it determined what kinds of forces to raise, what classes of ships to build, and which weapons and other war materiel to purchase. In addition, Congress could influence the war in other ways, such as by restricting trade, encouraging privateering, promoting enlistments in the army or navy, and determining how to finance the war effort.

The senior army officers who played the largest role in the field were Major General William Henry Harrison in the Old Northwest, Major General Andrew Jackson in the Old Southwest, and Major General Jacob Brown and Brigadier General Winfield Scott on the northern frontier, especially along the Niagara River. Although these men had to carry out policy directives from Washington, such was the distance of their operations from the capital that they had considerable latitude.

Captain Isaac Chauncey was the senior officer on the northern lakes and had immediate command of Lake Ontario, which was considered the most important of the lakes. Master Commandant Oliver Hazard Perry had command on Lake Erie, and Master Commandant Thomas Macdonough was in charge of Lake Champlain. Various naval captains, such as Isaac Hull, Stephen Decatur, and William Bainbridge, had command of one or more ocean-going warships that saw combat on the high seas.

4 | Who were the British war leaders?

The British government was dominated by three men: Lord Liverpool, who became prime minister in 1812; Lord Castlereagh, the foreign secretary; and the Duke of Wellington, who was campaigning in Spain but who was often consulted on significant issues. These men devoted little attention to the American problem because their attention was focused on Europe, where the British were locked in a titanic contest with France. Known as the French Revolutionary and Napoleonic Wars, this struggle lasted off and on from 1793 to 1815 and was far more important to the British than the American war because it determined which nation would dominate Europe and the wider world. Officials in the Admiralty and War Office made decisions affecting the course of the War of 1812, but they, too, had to focus on the more important war in Europe. Lord Bathurst, the secretary of state for war and the colonies, devoted more attention to the war with America but took his lead from Liverpool, who provided direction after consulting with Castlereagh, Wellington, and other officials.

In Canada, the British government relied on Sir George Prevost (usually pronounced Pray-vo), the governor of Canada and commander-in-chief of British forces in North America. Based on broad directives received from London, Prevost crafted a strategy to wage war against the United States. To carry out this strategy, Prevost had a number of experienced British officers in the field, most notably Major General Isaac Brock in the West, and Major General Roger H. Sheaffe and Lieutenant General Gordon Drummond on the Niagara front. On the Gulf Coast, Major General Edward Pakenham was in charge. Like their American counterparts, the British generals enjoyed considerable freedom of action because most of their operations were conducted far from policymakers in Quebec and London.

Commodore Sir James Yeo (pronounced Yo), the ranking Royal Navy officer in Canada, shaped the war on the northern lakes. He was in charge of Lake Ontario, while Commander Robert H. Barclay was in charge of Lake Erie, and Captain George Downie had command on Lake Champlain. Overseeing the war against the U.S. coast was a succession of naval officers assigned to the American station—Admiral Sir John Borlase Warren, Vice Admiral Sir Alexander Cochrane, and Rear Admiral George Cockburn.

To secure Indian assistance, the British depended on three native leaders. Two prominent Shawnee brothers, Tecumseh and Tenskwatawa (better known as the Prophet), built a pan-Indian alliance in the West that aided the British, while a Scottish-Cherokee mixed-blood, John Norton, became a Mohawk chief. In that capacity he helped keep the Grand River Iroquois loyal to the Crown and took part in most of the battles on the Niagara River.

5 | How was the War of 1812 related to the Napoleonic Wars?

It was a direct outgrowth. The British realized that if they lost the Napoleonic Wars they would surrender their independence and perhaps even their essential character. War with the young republic was always preferable to defeat at the hands of France. Hence, the British did not hesitate to adopt policies that furthered their war effort against France even if those policies risked war with the United States.

6 | What caused the War of 1812?

Tension grew primarily out of British maritime practices, particularly the Orders-in-Council and impressment. The Orders-in-Council limited American trade with the European Continent. Impressment was the Royal Navy's practice of removing seamen (often called "tars") from American merchant vessels on the high seas.

The British government issued the Orders-in-Council between 1807 and 1809 in response to French trade restrictions, known as the Continental Decrees, which sought to crush Britain economically by closing the Continent to British ships and goods. The Brit-

Sir George Prevost (1767–1816) served as governor-general of Canada during the War of 1812. Although he did a fine job of providing for the defense of Canada in the first two years of the contest, his domestic enemies triumphed over him because of his lack of success as a field commander. (Portrait by S. W. Reynolds. William Wood, ed., Select British Documents of the Canadian War of 1812.*)*

ish retaliated with their own decrees. Although their aim was to deny France and its allies the fruits of any trade from which they were excluded, the Orders had a direct impact on American trade with the Continent. Between 1807 and 1812, the Royal Navy, British privateers, and port officials seized some four hundred American merchant vessels, mostly for violating the Orders-in-Council. During this same period, France and its allies seized almost as many American ships.

The British impressed seamen from American merchant vessels to keep their navy adequately manned. The Royal Navy was a vital source of Britain's power and the only thing preventing a French invasion. During the European war its manpower needs soared, from 45,000 in 1793 to 145,000 in 1812. To adequately man its ships, the navy had to call upon all available British seamen. Although the Royal Navy claimed the right to impress only British subjects, many American sailors (perhaps 10,000 between 1793 and 1812) were caught in the dragnet. The British also upheld the doctrine of indelible allegiance and thus claimed the right to impress even those British subjects who had become naturalized American citizens. This caused little difficulty in practice because so few British seamen in the American merchant marine bothered to take out citizenship papers.

7 | What was a "protection"?

It was a document, comparable to a modern identification card or passport, that the U.S. government began issuing to American seamen in 1796 to protect them from impressment. Although officially called a certificate of citizenship, it was popularly known as "protection" because of its purpose. But photography had not yet been invented, and the document contained no portrait, only a description of the holder. Typically, it included the seaman's age, height, build, hair and eye color, and any distinguishing features. Such a description was vague enough to fit other people, and British seamen easily acquired the documents by theft, fraud, or purchase. As a result, most British naval officials refused to give any credence to the documents.

8 | What was the *Chesapeake* affair?

It was a British attack on a U.S. warship. Although the British did not normally claim the right to impress from foreign warships (which were considered an extension of a nation's sovereignty or territory), occasionally over-zealous Royal Navy officers insisted on doing so. On June 22, 1807, H.M. Ship *Leopard* (carrying 52 guns and commanded by Captain Salusbury Pryce Humphreys) approached the U.S. Frigate *Chesapeake* (40 guns, commanded by Captain James Barron) nine miles off the coast of Virginia. Acting on orders from his superior, Admiral Sir George Berkeley, who was then in charge of the British navy at the Halifax station, Humphreys demanded the right to search for four Royal Navy deserters known to be on board the American ship. (Of the four, three were actually American citizens who had been impressed into British service.)

When Barron refused to allow the search, the *Leopard* opened fire, killing or wounding nineteen of the American crew. The *Chesapeake* was unprepared for the attack, and Barron hauled down his flag, a sign of surrender. The British then boarded and removed the four deserters. Barron was later convicted by a court-martial of neglecting to prepare his ship for action and suspended from the service for five years.

The attack on the *Chesapeake* produced outrage in the United States. Great Britain disavowed the attack, but a settlement was delayed because the United States sought to use the affair to force the British to give up impressment altogether. Not until November 1811 was a settlement reached, and not until the following July (a month after the United States had declared war) did the British finally return two of the American seamen. (The third had died in captivity, and the British subject had been hanged.) For four years, the *Chesapeake* affair had festered, serving as a reminder to the American people of how lightly the Royal Navy regarded U.S. sovereignty.

9 | What was the *Little Belt* affair?

Essentially, retaliation for the *Chesapeake* affair. After the attack on the *Chesapeake*, the secretary of the navy explicitly ordered all U.S. warships to resist any searches and in 1811 dispatched the U.S. Frigate *President* (carrying 54 guns and commanded by Captain John Rodgers) to cruise the American coast to prevent similar incidents. On May 16, the *President* encountered H.M. Sloop *Little Belt*, mounting 20 guns and commanded by Captain Arthur Bingham. When neither commander could identify the opposing ship, they exchanged fire. The *Little Belt* was no match for the larger American frigate, and by the time the firing stopped there were thirty-two British casualties compared to only one American. The British chose not to make an issue of the incident, which most Americans saw as fitting payback for the *Chesapeake* affair.

10 | Was war the only way to force the British to change their policies?

Yes. In the years before the war, the young republic had tried to persuade both Britain and France to show greater respect for American rights by adopting a series of trade restrictions. Known collectively as the restrictive system, these measures included various non-importation and non-exportation laws, including an especially onerous and controversial embargo that lasted for fifteen months, from December 1807 to March 1809, and prohibited American ships and goods from leaving port. The restrictive system was an abject failure. It destroyed American prosperity and sharply reduced government revenue, which was heavily dependent upon trade, without winning any concessions from Britain or France.

11 | Does this mean that war was the only option for the United States?

Not necessarily. To Jeffersonian Republicans, the choices in 1812 were war, submission, or more trade restrictions, and most now believed that war was the best option. Federalists argued for peace and accommodation with Great Britain, a policy Republicans saw as nothing less than submission.

In a way, Republicans were the idealists of the age, determined to risk all to uphold their vision of freedom of the seas and to force an end to British practices they considered a threat to American sovereignty. They even dubbed the war "a second war of independence." Federalists, by contrast, were realists, willing to accept the world the way it was and make the best of what they conceded was a bad situation. "The question is not what we want," said a Virginia Federalist, "but what, under all circumstances, it is possible we can get."[1]

12 | What role did the "War Hawks" play in bringing on the war?

Theirs was a central role. The "War Hawks" were a dozen Republicans in the House of Representatives, headed by thirty-four-year-old Henry Clay of Kentucky, who pushed the war program through Congress. Clay, only recently elevated to the ceremonial post of Speaker, molded the office into a position of power. He kept the war movement on track by packing key committees, controlling debate, interpreting House rules, and in general holding recalcitrant members in line. The War Hawks also worked closely with President Madison and Secretary of State Monroe to advance their agenda.

13 | What was the Henry affair?

John Henry was a British spy who had gathered intelligence on the state of opinion in New England in 1808–1809 after the *Chesapeake* incident had generated a war scare. Unable to get the inflated compensation he demanded from the British government, Henry sold his papers to the U.S. government for the staggering sum of $50,000, which was the entire secret service budget. The administration sent the papers to Congress in March 1812 in the hope of fostering support for war and discrediting the opposition. But this sort of intelligence-gathering was commonplace whenever war threatened, and the papers revealed little that was damaging to Federalists. Federalists everywhere were irate that so much public money had been spent to so little purpose, and even Republicans had trouble mustering much indignation over Henry's mission.

14 | How close was the vote on the declaration of war?

Closer than the vote on any other formal declaration of war in American history. In the House of Representatives, the vote was 79–49, in the Senate 19–13. About 20 percent of the Republicans in Congress voted against the war; so, too, did every single Federalist. Assuming that members of Congress fairly represented their constituents, this means that almost 39 percent of the American people in 1812 opposed the decision to go to war. By contrast, the vote in Congress on every other formal declaration of war—against Mexico in 1846, Spain in 1898, Germany and Austria in 1917, and

Germany, Japan, and Italy in 1941—was unanimous or at least overwhelming.

15 | Why was there so much opposition to the war?

The reasoning of the dissidents varied, but most believed that the United States was unlikely to achieve its war aims against such a powerful foe. Britain, after all, considered her maritime practices vital to her dominion of the seas and thus crucial in her war effort against Napoleonic France. In addition, those who opposed war feared that the cost in blood and treasure might be too great to justify the decision. If their worst fears were realized, the government would be bankrupted, the economy destroyed, and the young and still fragile nation torn apart. Many Federalists, especially in New England, also feared that a British war would lead to an alliance with France and eventually French domination. According to William E. Channing, a Massachusetts clergyman, French dominion threatened not just American wealth, but *the minds, the character, the morals, [and] the religion of our nation.*[2]

Once the die was cast for war, most anti-war Republicans fell into line. Federalists did not. With hard-line New Englanders leading the way, Federalists continued to denounce the war after it had been declared.

16 | Did Republicans tolerate this opposition?

Only reluctantly. Before the war, Republican leaders had repeatedly said they would brook no opposition once war was declared, and as a result there were pro-war riots in several Republican cities. Mobs in 1812 assaulted Federalist editors in Savannah, Georgia, and in Norristown, Pennsylvania, ultimately driving both newspapers out of business. In Baltimore a particularly vicious series of riots destroyed the offices of the anti-war *Federal Republican* newspaper. Among the Federalist casualties of the Baltimore riots were the paper's editor, Alexander Contee Hanson, and "Light-Horse" Harry Lee, a hero of the Revolution and the father of Robert E. Lee. Both men never recovered from internal injuries they sustained from an enraged and drunken Republican mob.

17 | Did Republican violence silence the Federalists?

Far from it. Although Federalists in the Republican-dominated middle and southern states became more circumspect in their opposition, New England Federalists, furious with the attempt to suppress free speech, dug in their heels. "The war," said the *Connecticut Courant*, "pretendedly for the freedom of the seas, is valiantly waged against the freedom of the press."[3] Federalists everywhere took out subscriptions to the *Federal Republican* to show their support, and thus the paper was more widely read after the riots than before. Finally, a public backlash against the violence, particularly in Maryland and states to the north, contributed to Federalist gains in the elections of 1812. Thus, in the end, the violent attempt to silence opponents of the war only added fuel to the anti-war fire

18 | What was the American plan for winning the war?

The United States could not challenge Britain on the high seas. The Royal Navy was too formidable for that. But Canada, which had only 500,000 people compared to 7.7 million in the United States, was vulnerable. The United States hoped to conquer most, if not all, of Canada and hold it for ransom on the maritime issues. If the British made no concessions on those issues, then presumably the United States would keep the conquered territory as a consolation prize.

There were some Americans, especially in the West, who saw the conquest and annexation of Canada as a primary war aim, and the administration never clearly spelled out its plans for Canada, probably to keep all of its options open. Henry Clay, who was himself a westerner, clarified American policy in a comment he made in late 1813. "Canada was not the end but the means," he said, "the object of the War being the redress of [maritime] injuries, and Canada being the instrument by which that redress was to be obtained."[4]

19 | Where was the war fought?

Because the United States targeted Canada, most of the fighting took place along the Canadian-American border. But because the British navy retaliated against the Atlantic coast, there was also considerable action on the American seaboard, especially in the Chesapeake, and several key engagements on the Gulf Coast, particularly at New Orleans. There was also fighting in the Old Southwest against the Creek Indians. In addition, American and British warships and privateers waged war and plundered one another's commerce on the high seas.

20 | How did the opposing armies stack up?

The Americans had around 12,000 regulars at the beginning of the war, but this was not much of a fighting force. The officer corps, which included many political appointees, lacked experience and professionalism. Winfield Scott characterized the majority of his fellow officers as "imbeciles and ignoramuses."[5] That was surely an exaggeration, although there was some truth in his assessment. The enlisted men were no better. Few had much training or combat experience.

The Americans could also draw on some 725,000 militia, but

citizen-soldiers had little training or military experience and could be called out only for short periods of service, usually three months. Unless steadied by the presence of regulars, they were unreliable in the heat of battle. The United States could count on some Indian allies as well, although not nearly so many as the British. For waging offensive warfare, the Americans simply could not field a very effective army.

Britain, by contrast, had developed a first-class army. Twenty years of warfare with France had produced a professional officer corps and a reliable complement of enlisted men. But because of commitments elsewhere, particularly in the Spanish Peninsula, the British had only about 10,000 regulars in Canada at the beginning of the War of 1812 and could ill afford to send many more until the war in Europe was over. The British could also draw on some 86,000 militia in Canada, although most were no more reliable than their American counterparts and were thus best used in support of regulars.

The British could also count on several thousand Indian warriors. Most Indians in eastern North America sided with the British to counter the relentless pressure and abuse of land-hungry Americans. Indian allies were a significant asset. They were good at scouting, tracking, and skirmishing, and, because of their penchant for torturing prisoners, their presence on the battlefield could tip the balance by inspiring terror in the enemy.

In sum, for waging the kind of defensive warfare needed to secure Canada, the British could field a pretty capable force, one likely to prevail against an inexperienced foe.

21 | What kinds of weapons did the armies use?

The standard shoulder arm used by both armies was the single-shot, muzzle-loaded, smooth-bore musket, which was accurate up to 100 yards but could be lethal at 200 yards. Although American troops used some muskets imported from Britain or France, the domestically manufactured Springfield Model 1795 was more common. This musket fired a .65 caliber ball, that is, a ball that was .65 inches in diameter. The British used a comparable weapon. This was the Land Pattern or Tower musket, more commonly called the "Brown Bess." The version in common use in 1812 was the India Pattern, which fired a .71 caliber ball.

Both sides also employed rifles, although these were far less common because they were less dependable in the field than muskets and slower to load. Their great advantage was their range. Because they had a grooved barrel, they were accurate up to 250 yards. In the United States, riflemen serving in regular units were issued the Harpers Ferry Model 1803, which fired a .54 caliber ball, or rifles made to a multitude of specifications by private contractors. Many volunteer militiamen in the West brought their own versions, known as Pennsylvania or Kentucky rifles. Although rifles were made to many different specifications, a typical one fired a .45 caliber ball. British rifle units were issued the Baker rifle, which fired a .625 caliber ball.

Regulars in both armies also carried bayonets (although the longer bayonets issued to riflemen were usually called "swords"). Armies did not often come in close enough contact to use their bayonets. Bayonet wounds were most common in night engagements, either because one army surprised the other or the opposing armies blundered into one another in the darkness. Officers usually carried muzzle-loaded pistols, but side arms played only a marginal role in combat.

For field artillery, both armies carried small iron or brass guns that fired solid or round shot (cannon balls) that typically weighed from three to twelve pounds but could weigh as much as eighteen or even twenty-four pounds. Round shot that was heated in a portable furnace was called "hot shot" and was useful for igniting a fire in a fort, building, or ship. Both sides also used howitzers and mortars, which fired exploding shells at an upward angle, and were useful for firing over friendly troops, hitting enemy troops on the reverse slope of a hill, or firing into fortifications. The British added a wrinkle by filling their shells with small iron balls known as "shrapnel" (named after its inventor, Lieutenant Henry Shrapnel).

For close action up to 300 yards, cannons and howitzers could fire case shot (also called canister), an iron or tin can filled with small iron balls and occasionally grapeshot, which was a canvas bag of iron balls weighing from 4 to 32 ounces each. Upon firing, the can or canvas disintegrated, releasing a deadly spray of metal.

In some engagements, the British used a new weapon they had devised, Congreve rockets. These resembled skyrockets in that a warhead loaded with combustible materials, solid shot, canister, or shrapnel was hurled toward the enemy by a propellant from an attached tube. Although the rockets had a launching stick that was supposed to provide stability, the weapons were wildly inaccurate. But such was their novelty on the battlefield that sometimes they panicked even seasoned troops.

22 | How were the armies supplied?

Only with great difficulty. Armies traveled on their stomachs, and getting food and other necessities to the Canadian-American frontier, where the bulk of the forces served, was a stupendous task. The wilderness was dense, the weather could be harsh, and the roads were crude. In addition, the local population was usually too small to support the influx of troops. Whenever possible, supplies were moved over waterways, but weather or enemy operations could make their use dangerous if not impossible.

Both armies struggled with logistical problems. As a result, the troops often did without, which usually increased looting and rates of desertion. Sometimes the outcome of an entire campaign turned on the success or failure of the supply service.

The United States had a much larger population to draw upon near the border and also enjoyed shorter and more secure lines of transportation. Most supplies moved from New York City to Albany and then north or west, or from Philadelphia to Pittsburgh and then on to the frontier. But the system never worked smoothly. Poor planning, a flawed administrative structure, and a shortage of cash often conspired with Mother Nature to slow or halt the flow of supplies to the armies that needed them.

For the British, the logistical challenges were greater. Despite a plentitude of cash, almost everything, even food, had to be shipped into Canada, much of it from the mother country 3,000 miles away. Supplies flowed up the St. Lawrence River and then to the fronts on the northern lakes. But the St. Lawrence and the lakes were in a battle zone and thus exposed to enemy interdiction. The British also had to supply not only their own troops but thousands of Indian allies and their dependents as well. The needs of the natives alone sometimes overwhelmed the British commissariat.

23 | How did the opposing navies compare?

Great Britain—long known as "Mistress of the Seas"—had undisputed naval superiority. She had 584 ships in commission in 1812, but they were scattered all over the world, performing blockade, convoy, or supply duty as well as a host of other tasks deemed essential to the war against Napoleonic France. As a result, the only ships available for immediate service in the American war in the summer of 1812 were those attached to the Halifax squadron. There were twenty-five ships in this squadron: one small ship-of-the-line (or battleship), five frigates (comparable to modern cruisers), and nineteen smaller vessels.

The United States had only sixteen warships in 1812—seven

frigates and nine smaller vessels—but the navy benefited from the nation's rich maritime tradition. The ships were well designed and well made, the officer corps capable, and the seamen experienced. Ship for ship and man for man, the republic's navy matched up well against the mighty Royal Navy.

The frigates were at the heart of the U.S. Navy. Although frigates were usually rated to carry thirty-six guns, the United States had three frigates of a new design—the *Constitution,* the *President,* and the *United States*—that were rated to carry forty-four guns but usually carried fifty or more. They were the most powerful cruisers in the world, capable of outmaneuvering and outfighting any other frigates and outrunning anything larger.

24 | What kinds of weapons did the navies use?

Both navies relied on artillery, mainly long guns, which usually ranged from 9- to 42-pounders. These guns fired solid shot, and at close range case or canister as well as grapeshot. Most warships also carried carronades, powerful short-range guns, the biggest of which were known as "smashers" because they could fire solid shot weighing as much as 68 pounds that could (because of slow muzzle velocity) blast apart even the thick oak hull of a large warship. Some warships also carried howitzers. British bomb ships were equipped with mortars, howitzers, and Congreve rockets. The largest of the mortars had a range of 3,000 yards, which was greater than that of any other weapon of the era.

American warships often carried specialized ordnance, such as bar or chain shot (two iron balls connected by a bar or chain) or star shot (five iron bars connected to a ring), for dismasting a ship or destroying its sails and rigging. Ships that lost their main mast, or sometimes even a secondary mast, could not maneuver and had to surrender.

Warships also employed sharpshooters from the "tops," that is, the platforms high up the masts. Small arms came into greater play if there was a boarding and hand-to-hand combat, but most naval battles were decided by artillery, usually long guns and carronades.

25 | How were warships at sea supplied?

They usually packed enough food, water, munitions, repair materials, and spare parts for a cruise, which typically was planned for three months but could last for as long as six. When they ran short of food or water or needed minor repairs that could not be done at sea, they stopped at a friendly port. When they needed major repairs, they had to find a naval yard that could perform them. That usually meant returning to a home port.

26 | What kind of medical treatment did the sick and wounded receive?

It was crude at best. There was little understanding of the importance of cleanliness, or of how to combat disease or control infection. Army and navy surgeons embraced the "heroic" practice of medicine, which meant that they bled and blistered patients or subjected them to assorted emetics, cathartics, and diuretics designed to purge the body of disease. The only way they knew to control infection or the spread of gangrene was to amputate the affected limb, an operation that had to be performed without the benefit of an anesthetic and often resulted in still more infection. Most patients subjected to an amputation were given a dose of spirits and a musket ball to bite. Hence, the phrase "to bite the bullet," which means having to do something unpleasant.

There were few effective drugs. The one most commonly used—known as the "Samson of the Materia Medica"—was calomel (mercurous chloride), a mercury compound that had no real therapeutic value. It was strictly a toxin that could only injure or even kill the patient. Sick or wounded soldiers often survived in spite of rather than because of the treatment they received.

27 | How were prisoners of war treated?

Reasonably well by the standards of the day, but there were many complaints, especially from enlisted men. Officers were considered gentlemen and were usually paroled to a nearby town (if they promised not to flee) or even sent home (if they promised not to serve again until exchanged). Militiamen were usually sent home on parole, too, because they were considered amateur soldiers. Enlisted men, however, were incarcerated until exchanged. The exchange rate that the two nations agreed upon reflected the caste system in the armed services: major generals and rear admirals were worth thirty privates; non-commissioned and petty officers were worth two.

The United States favored penitentiaries in states like Massachusetts and Kentucky that were near (but not too near) the northern border. The British had large prison complexes on Melville Island at Halifax and in Dartmoor, England. They also used prison ships docked at ports in Canada, Great Britain, and the West Indies. Most Americans taken by the British were privateersmen, and the British refused to exchange them unless their ships carried at least fourteen guns.

The prisons were usually dark, dank, and unhealthy, and the prison ships were worse. Most prisoners were not given enough food to maintain their weight, and they had to contend with malnutrition, disease, and abuse. The British had a reputation for being especially hard on privateersmen to induce them to join the Royal Navy, but not many succumbed. Most prisoners languished in prison for months if not years, and many perished from disease before being exchanged or released at the end of the war.

The Battle of Tippecanoe ignited an Indian war in the Old Northwest that blended into the War of 1812 seven months later. As this illustration suggests, the combat was close and deadly. (Print by Kurz & Allison. Library of Congress.)

28 | How was the Battle of Tippecanoe related to the War of 1812?

It was the first battle in an Indian war in the Old Northwest that blended into the War of 1812. William Henry Harrison had been appointed governor of the Indiana Territory in 1800 and two years later was given authority over the Indians in the region. In the years that followed, he imposed a series of dubious land cession treaties on the Indians, culminating in 1809 in the Treaty of Fort Wayne, which transferred 2.5 million acres on the Wabash River to the United States. Harrison's land grab infuriated a growing number of natives living in the region.

Spearheading the opposition were the two Shawnees, the Prophet and Tecumseh, who together built a formidable religious movement and military alliance to resist the adoption of white culture and the loss of land. The center of their resistance was Prophet's Town, an Indian village established close to the confluence of the Tippecanoe and Wabash rivers near present-day Lafayette, Indiana. Determined to break up this settlement, Harrison marched to Prophet's Town with 1,000 regulars and volunteer militia in the fall of 1811.

After he had made camp near the village, Harrison was attacked in the early morning hours of November 7 by some 500 Indians, mostly Kickapoos, Winnebagoes, and Potawatomis, under the leadership of the Prophet. Harrison suffered heavy casualties, 200 killed and wounded, double the Indian losses, but he drove the natives from the field, burned Prophet's Town and much of the Indians' food, and claimed victory.

The Battle of Tippecanoe was the first engagement of an Indian war that was fought in earnest for two years. Tippecanoe drove wavering tribes into the British camp and ensured that when the War of 1812 began seven months later, most Indians in the Old Northwest would side with Great Britain.

CHAPTER TWO

The First Invasion of Canada

29 | What was Canada like in 1812?

Canada consisted of Britain's six North American provinces: Upper Canada (which is now Ontario), Lower Canada (which today is Quebec), Nova Scotia, New Brunswick, Prince Edward Island, and Cape Breton Island. Newfoundland had a separate status. The population of Canada in 1812 was about 500,000. That population consisted of descendants of the original French inhabitants; British immigrants, including refugees from the American Revolution who were known as "United Empire Loyalists"; and recent American immigrants drawn to Canada by free land and low taxes who were optimistically called "Late Loyalists." The British immigrants, particularly the Loyalists, were the only group whose fidelity the mother country could count on.

Canada in 1812 was often compared to a tree. The tap roots were the sea lanes that extended from the Gulf of St. Lawrence to Great Britain and thus linked Canada to the mother country. This was a vital supply route because Canadians were not self-sufficient and imported many British goods. The trunk of the Canadian tree was the St. Lawrence River, which linked the Gulf of St. Lawrence to the Great Lakes. Because of the dense wilderness that covered the land, virtually everything sent to the Canadian interior moved up the St. Lawrence River. Two cities, Quebec and Montreal, anchored British defenses on this vital waterway. The branches of the Canadian tree were the scattered settlements on the Great Lakes and nearby rivers.

30 | What was the best way to conquer Canada?

There were only two ways to do it. One might attempt to seal off Canada from the rest of the world by severing the tap roots, that is, deploy a squadron of warships to the Gulf of St. Lawrence to stop all trade with the mother country, but that was not possible when Great Britain controlled the seas. The next best option was to sever the Canadian trunk by seizing control of the St. Lawrence River, which meant capturing Montreal and Quebec. Montreal might be taken, but Quebec—well fortified on a cliff, and in the summer months accessible to the Royal Navy—was nearly impregnable. The United States would have to settle for taking control of the St. Lawrence at Montreal. Creating a choke point there would deprive all settlements to the west of vital supplies and probably force them to seek terms. It would also leave Quebec in British hands and present a powerful threat to the rear.

31 | Did Republicans think that the conquest of Canada would be easy?

Yes. Thomas Jefferson thought that taking most of Canada would be "a mere matter of marching," and he was far from alone.[6] Republicans assumed that the residents of Canada would greet their American cousins as liberators and offer little resistance. John Randolph of Virginia, a fierce Republican critic of the war, accused the war party of expecting "a holiday campaign." With "no expense of blood or treasure on our part," he said, "Canada is to conquer herself—she is to be subdued by the principles of fraternity."[7]

32 | What was American strategy in 1812?

American leaders recognized the importance of striking at the

Canadian trunk, but without the support of Federalist New England they doubted that such a campaign would succeed. Hence, they shifted the focus of their operations to the West. That would enable them to take advantage of western support for the war and to target not only the British but also their western Indian allies, who had stepped up their raids on American frontier settlements after Tippecanoe. Unfortunately, it also meant that the United States would fritter away its limited resources flaying at the branches on the Canadian tree.

Relying on regulars and militia, the administration's plan was to launch a three-pronged invasion. One army would invade across the Detroit River in the West, a second army would cross the Niagara River in the center, and a third would follow the Lake Champlain–Richelieu River corridor into Canada in order to threaten Montreal.

33 | What was British strategy in 1812?

Mostly defensive, and for several reasons. First, although the British had a respectable regular force in Canada, the Americans could draw on a much larger pool of manpower to increase their army and a much larger stockpile of food and other necessities to keep those troops supplied. Secondly, the British could ill afford to divert forces from the more important war in Europe to North America. Finally, the British hoped that the repeal of the Orders-in-Council, which coincided with the American declaration of war, would make peace possible once the news reached the United States. Until it did, they were anxious to avoid any operations that might provoke anger and prolong the war. They were, however, willing to exploit any offensive opportunity that might present itself. Their best opportunity for such an offensive came on the Detroit River frontier in the late summer of 1812.

34 | What happened on the Detroit River front?

Brigadier General William Hull, an aging Revolutionary War veteran who suffered from various health problems, laboriously cut a road through Ohio to reach Detroit early in July. With a mixed force of some 2,000 regulars and militia, Hull had a numerical advantage over the 1,600 British regulars, militia, and Indians he faced, but he was reluctant to attack the British stronghold, Fort Amherstburg, across the river. He was also beset by supply problems and had no stomach for battle anyway, and when he learned that Fort Mackinac to the north had fallen, he lost his resolve altogether.

35 | How did the British capture Fort Mackinac?

Through quick action, superior force, and stealth. Fort Mackinac was located on an island in the strait that connected Lake Michigan and Lake Huron. It was lightly defended by Lieutenant Porter Hanks and sixty men who did not know that war had been declared. The British realized the importance of the fort for controlling Indians in the region, and, after some vacillation, General Isaac Brock authorized Captain Charles Roberts, who was in command of nearby Fort St. Joseph, to attack. Roberts pulled together a motley force of 625 men, mainly Indians, and sailed to Mackinac in some canoes and a schooner owned by the North West Company. Arriving at Mackinac early on the morning of July 17, Roberts dragged two small field pieces to the heights that commanded the American fort and demanded that Hanks surrender. The American officer had little choice but to comply.

Overleaf: The War in the North

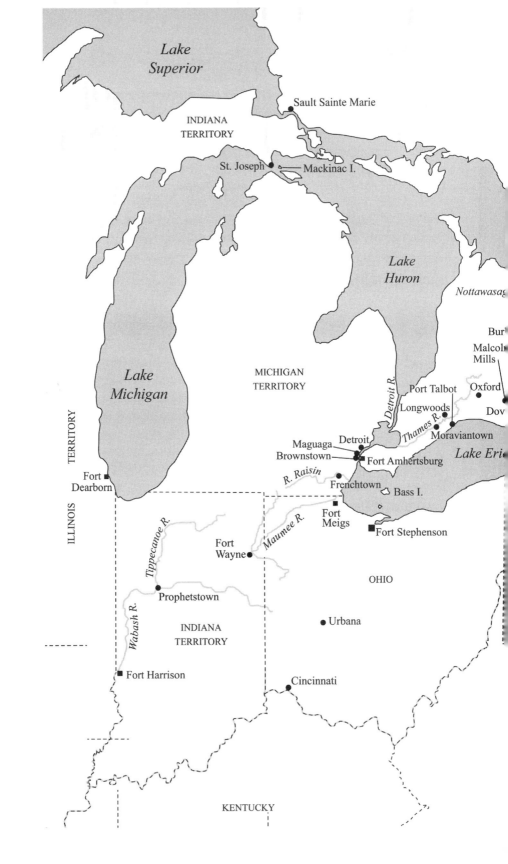

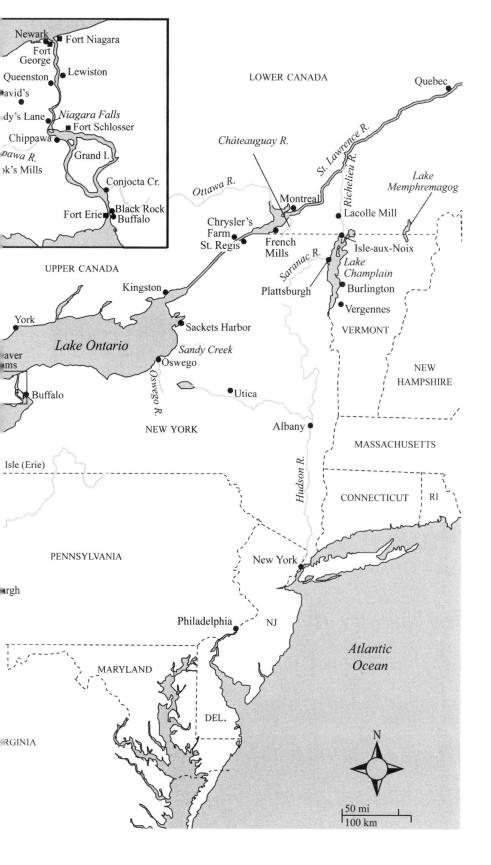

36 | How did General Hull respond to the fall of Mackinac?

He panicked. Convinced that the loss of the fort "opened the northern hive of Indians, and they were swarming down in every direction," he withdrew into Fort Detroit and became increasingly distracted and desperate.[8] His British counterpart, General Brock, who now had an army about equal to Hull's, laid siege and hinted that he might not be able to control his Indian allies if forced to attack. In response, Hull, who feared an Indian massacre, surrendered his entire force on August 16. He later claimed that he was nearly out of gunpowder, but a British inventory after the surrender showed otherwise. Hull surrendered not because of a lack of war materiel but because he lost his nerve.

37 | What was the Fort Dearborn Massacre?

It was a bloody byproduct of Hull's panic at Fort Detroit. When Hull learned of the fall of Mackinac, he ordered Captain Nathan Heald to evacuate Fort Dearborn, located in present-day Chicago. Heald had sixty-five regulars and militia and was responsible for two dozen civilians as well. Although the fort was defensible and the nearby Potawatomi Indians were known to be unfriendly, Heald was determined to obey his orders. The Potawatomis agreed not to molest the Americans but became furious when they learned that a promise to give them all the public property in the fort did not include war materiel and liquor. On August 15, after the Americans had left the safety of the fort, 500 Indians, mostly Potawatomis under the leadership of Blackbird, attacked, killing most of the Americans, including some who had surrendered.

The Potawatomis bore a particular grudge against William Wells, a "white Indian" who had once lived with the Miamis. After returning to white society, Wells had played a role in Harrison's dubious land cession treaties and then had stolen part of the Indians' annuities. The Potawatomis now took their revenge (and also showed their respect) by cutting off Wells's head, carving out his heart, and eating it raw.

38 | How did the United States try to retrieve the situation in the Old Northwest?

William Henry Harrison, immensely popular because he was a fellow westerner who had been successful at Tippecanoe in 1811, succeeded the disgraced William Hull. In the fall of 1812, Harrison spent enormous sums of money building a new army and stockpiling supplies. The administration pressed for a winter campaign to regain control of the Old Northwest, but a rainy fall made most of the roads impassable, and the only operations launched produced mixed results. One American force prevailed against the Miamis at Mississinewa in Indiana Territory in December, but another suffered a disastrous defeat at the hands of an Anglo-Indian force at Frenchtown in Michigan Territory in January.

39 | What was the Battle of Mississinewa?

In late November 1812, Harrison dispatched some 600 regulars, volunteers, and militia under Lieutenant Colonel John B. Campbell from Ohio to destroy a group of Miami villages on the Mississinewa River in present-day Indiana. On December 17, Campbell attacked one village, killing or capturing close to fifty Indians. He also destroyed several nearby villages that by now had been abandoned. The following morning before daybreak, some 300 Indians launched a furious counterattack against Campbell's fortified camp. After an hour of heavy fighting, dawn broke and Campbell launched his own counterattack with mounted troops that drove the Indians off. The United States sustained around sixty killed and wounded, although a great many more suffered from frostbite during the march to and from the battle site. Indian losses are unknown but were probably larger. The Battle of Mississinewa is sometimes portrayed as the first American land victory of the war, although no British were involved.

40 | What was the Battle of Frenchtown?

Although Harrison was not ready to undertake further offensive operations, an advance force under Brigadier General James Winchester at the rapids of the Maumee River (near present-day Perrysburg, Ohio) learned that an Anglo-Indian force threatened Frenchtown (now Monroe, Michigan) about forty miles away. In response to the plea from the residents for protection, Winchester sent 700 men, who drove off the enemy in an engagement on January 18, 1813.

Winchester arrived soon after with another 300 men and took charge, but he ignored the danger that the enemy's main force, only twenty-two miles away at Fort Amherstburg, might counterattack and did not deploy his own men to the best advantage. He was caught by surprise when Colonel Henry Procter attacked on January 22 with some 1,200 regulars, militia, and Indians. Both commanders showed poor judgment in the bloody encounter that followed, but ultimately Winchester was captured and surrendered what was left of his force to avoid an Indian massacre (much as Hull had done five months earlier at Detroit). The United States probably suffered close to 350 killed and wounded; the British and their Indian allies around 200.

41 | What was the River Raisin Massacre?

The American surrender at Frenchtown was followed by another disaster long remembered in the West. Fearing a counterattack after his success at Frenchtown, Procter withdrew precipitously, leaving the American prisoners at the mercy of vengeful Indians. The day after the battle, drunken Indians killed a number of the prisoners—probably around thirty—in what was bitterly recalled in the United States as the "River Raisin Massacre." Americans saw the massacre not simply as a reflection of Indian savagery but also as proof of British complicity in the atrocities.

42 | What happened on the Niagara front?

The American in charge of the invasion here was a New York militia officer, Major General Stephen Van Rensselaer. Known as "the last of the Patroons," Van Rensselaer was wealthy and influential but had no combat experience. Hence, he relied on his younger cousin, Colonel Solomon Van Rensselaer, a veteran of the Indian wars of the 1790s. The ranking regular army officer on this front was Brigadier General Alexander Smyth, a vain and pompous blowhard who was reluctant to cooperate with any militia officer who outranked him. Nevertheless, the Van Rensselaers were determined to press ahead with their operation. The result was the Battle of Queenston Heights.

43 | What happened in the Battle of Queenston Heights?

On October 13 the younger Van Rensselaer led an advance force of 300 men across the Niagara River. Van Rensselaer was wounded four or five times and was knocked out of action. Other troops came

As this illustration suggests, Americans were convinced that the British were behind the atrocities committed by Indians in the West. In truth, the British tried to restrain their Indian allies, although not always successfully. (Watercolor etching by William Charles. Library of Congress.)

across, but the entire American force was pinned down at the riverbank until a fisherman's path was discovered that led to Queenston Heights above. This gave the Americans a commanding position, but they desperately needed reinforcements to hold their ground.

The senior Van Rensselaer could not persuade militia on the American side of the river to cross over. The militia based their refusal on the Constitution, claiming they could not be forced to serve outside the United States, but more likely they had been spooked by the war whoops they heard across the river and by the sight of the dead and wounded on their way to the rear who were paraded in front of them.

Without reinforcements, the position of the Americans on the heights became increasingly precarious. They were relentlessly harassed by a band of Grand River Iroquois under the Mohawk leader John Norton while the British gathered their forces for a counterattack. Although General Brock was killed early in that attack, the British, now led by General Roger H. Sheaffe, forced Lieutentant Colonel Winfield Scott, who had taken command of the American force on the heights, to surrender. The Americans lost close to 1,200 men killed, wounded, or captured. British and Indian losses, by contrast, were only about 150.

44 | Why didn't the United States follow up with another attack on the Niagara?

General Alexander Smyth assumed command of the American army after the debacle at Queenston Heights. He issued bombastic proclamations promising to renew the attack, but the season was late, the element of surprise was gone, and Smyth showed no talent for managing amphibious operations. On November 25, Smyth sent two advance parties across to attack British batteries and destroy a bridge near Fort Erie, but they were only partly successful, and Smyth ultimately called off the attack. This ended the campaign on the Niagara frontier.

45 | What happened on the Lake Champlain– Richelieu River front?

Given the importance of this theater, surprisingly little of consequence. The man in charge of this part of the invasion was another Revolutionary War relic who had lost his taste for battle. Major General Henry Dearborn preferred to devote his limited energy to recruiting and tending to the defenses of New York, and planned to leave the actual campaigning to his junior officers. But when Brigadier General Joseph Bloomfield became ill, Dearborn was forced to take charge. By then it was mid-November, and the American army of about 6,000 regulars and militia had departed from Plattsburgh. Dearborn caught up with the army on the Canadian-American border.

Dearborn gave Colonel Zebulon Pike, the celebrated explorer, authority to take 500 regulars to attack an Indian camp. Unable to locate the camp, Pike found an Anglo-Indian stronghold on the Lacolle River that he assaulted instead. Pike drove the British and their Indian allies off, but in the confusion the Americans fired on each other. Although the Battle of Lacolle Mill ended in a modest American victory, Dearborn decided to call off the campaign when he learned that most of his militia units would not cross the frontier. A Republican later described Dearborn's failure as a "miscarriage without even [the] heroism of disaster."[9]

46 | Why did the American campaign fail?

A combination of factors. The Americans suffered from inept leadership, inexperienced regulars, undependable militia, and intractable supply problems. They also faced a formidable foe. The small British force charged with defending Canada was a determined and tough opponent and enjoyed crucial assistance from Indian allies. In addition, the British controlled both Lake Erie and Lake Ontario, which facilitated the movement of men and supplies to the western fronts.

There was another reason: The response of the inhabitants of Canada was far different from what many Republicans had expected. Although some American immigrants welcomed the invasion, and many French and even some British residents were indifferent, the Loyalists who had migrated to Canada from the United States after the American Revolution were fiercely loyal to the British Crown, and they provided a core around which others could rally.

In addition, early British success in the war stiffened popular resolve. "The militia have been inspired . . . with confidence," reported General Isaac Brock after the fall of Detroit. "The disaffected are silenced."[10] Canadian militiamen saw considerable combat early in the war and later performed a host of essential support tasks for British regulars.

47 | What happened to the American commanders responsible for the failure?

Hull was paroled by the British and returned to the United States, where he was court-martialed and convicted of cowardice and neglect of duty. He was sentenced to be shot, but the court recommended leniency because of his Revolutionary War service and his age. President Madison followed this recommendation, and Hull spent his remaining days (until his death in 1825) trying to defend his actions at Detroit.

Stephen Van Rensselaer resigned his command. Although subsequently defeated for the governorship of New York, he remained active in public life and played an important role in establishing the Erie Canal. His successor on the Niagara, Alexander Smyth, was so unpopular with the troops that they took pot shots at his tent, forcing him to leave the camp. In 1813 he was dropped from the rolls of the army without the courtesy of a hearing. Henry Dearborn, by contrast, retained his command for another year until additional military setbacks forced the administration to reassign him to other duties.

48 | How did the U.S. Navy perform in 1812?

Exceptionally well. The greatest achievement of the U.S. Navy is also the one that is least appreciated: It prevented the Royal Navy from blockading the American coast in the first six months of the war. The only ships the British could deploy against the United States in the summer of 1812 were those stationed at Halifax under the command first of Vice Admiral Herbert Sawyer and then of Admiral Sir John Borlase Warren.

When Admiral Sawyer learned that war had been declared, he planned to post a single British warship in front of each American port to intercept American merchant vessels that were then racing back to port, their holds bursting with foreign goods. But when he learned that the United States had sent some of its warships to sea in a squadron, he feared that his blockading ships might be knocked off one at a time. He therefore kept his squadron together and made a single sweep through American waters, bagging few prizes in the process. Hundreds of American merchant vessels got safely back into port. The goods they brought replenished American stockpiles and the taxes paid on those imports boosted government revenue. The returning ships also provided large numbers of experienced seamen for the privateers and warships that were then fitting out for action.

49 | Did the U.S. Navy win any battles in 1812?

Yes, it did, and they were impressive. In fact, the United States won the first five single-ship engagements of the war. Most spectacular were three battles won by the heavy frigates.

With Captain Isaac Hull in command, the *Constitution* (carrying 55 guns) demonstrated its fine sailing qualities and the superb seamanship of its crew when it escaped from the Halifax squadron in a celebrated fifty-seven-hour chase. A month later, on August 19, still under Hull's command, the *Constitution* defeated the British frigate *Guerrière* (49 guns), Captain James R. Dacres (pronounced Day-kers) commanding. Then on October 25, the U.S. Frigate *United States,* carrying 56 guns and commanded by Captain Stephen Decatur, defeated the British frigate *Macedonian,* which was carrying

49 guns and was commanded by Captain John S. Carden. Decatur added to his laurels by bringing the captured British ship into an American port as a prize of war. On December 29, the *Constitution* completed the American hat trick. Now carrying 54 guns and commanded by Captain William Bainbridge, she defeated the British frigate *Java*, 49 guns, commanded by Captain Henry Lambert.

50 | How did the U.S. Frigate *Constitution* get its nickname?

According to Moses Smith, a seaman on the *Constitution*, the ship got its nickname in 1812 during the engagement with the *Guerrière*. After watching enemy solid shot bounce off the thick twenty-two-inch oak hull, one of the American sailors cried out: "Huzza! Her sides are made of iron!"[11] The nickname "Ironsides" took hold, and by 1813 the ship was already affectionately known as "Old Ironsides."

51 | What was the significance of the American naval victories?

They had no strategic importance. Defeating a few British warships did not cut into British naval power in any meaningful way, nor did it have much of an impact on the course of the war. Nevertheless, these victories were greeted with a huge roar of approval in the United States. Not only did they offset the dismal news from the Canadian frontier, they showed that the young republic could do something that no other nation had done in recent memory—humble the mighty Mistress of the Seas.

The victories also convinced a number of Republicans of the benefits of naval power. Congress, which had refused to expand the navy on the eve of the war, now launched a major construction program to add more heavy frigates and even some ships-of-the-line

The U.S. Frigate Constitution *began her great run as a warship and earned the nickname "Old Ironsides" with her victory over the British frigate* Guerrière *in 1812. (Painting by T. Birch; engraving by C. Tiebout. Library of Congress.)*

to the republic's naval inventory. Although none of those ships were finished before the war's end, the legislation demonstrated a new commitment to maintaining a large navy that could better protect the nation's coast and commerce.

News of the defeats at sea went down hard in Great Britain. In some twenty years of warfare with France and her allies, the number of times the British had lost ship-to-ship duels could be counted on one hand. The British greeted the string of American victories with a combination of shock, indignation, and puzzlement. In truth, there was no mystery to the outcome of these naval duels, nor was there any disgrace in the British defeats. The heavier frigates had hulls that were thicker than those of conventional frigates and thus were better able to withstand enemy fire. They also carried a complement of 24-pounder guns rather than the usual 18-pounders. In short, the opposing ships were far from equal, and in each engagement, as one would expect, the more powerful ship prevailed.

Publicly, the British claimed that the American frigates were ships-of-the-line in disguise, which was untrue. Privately, the Admiralty ordered British frigates to avoid single-ship duels with their larger American counterparts. This made good sense because the heavy frigates were so much more powerful than conventional frigates. The British also launched a crash program to create some heavy frigates of their own, either by cutting down existing ships-of-the-line or by building new ones. By the end of the war, they had a dozen in service, although most had been built so hastily that they were still no match for the American frigates, nor were they a useful long-term addition to the Royal Navy.

52 | What role did American privateers play in 1812?

A significant one. Merchants were quick to convert their fastest commercial vessels into privateers by arming them, boosting the size of their crews, and securing the necessary government papers to cruise against the enemy's commerce. Catching the British unawares, American privateers made 450 prizes in the first six months of the war.

Among the most successful privateers were the *Yankee* (15 guns), sailing out of Bristol, Rhode Island, which took eight British vessels valued at $300,000, and the *Rossie* (15 guns), commanded by Joshua Barney of Baltimore, which captured eighteen prizes reportedly worth $1.5 million. Although most privateers operated off the coast of Canada or in the Caribbean, they could be found almost anywhere in the world. "[American] privateers," complained a contributor to the British *Naval Chronicle* in early 1813, "have roved with impunity and success to all corners of the earth."[12] These privateers could not win the war, but they cost British merchants considerable money, drove up marine insurance rates, and, like the Navy's victories, produced considerable pride in America and anger in Britain.

53 | Were there any British privateers?

Yes, there were. Although American privateers have received most of the attention, British privateers, many operating from Canadian ports, were also active. Privateers sailing from ports in New Brunswick and Nova Scotia enjoyed the most success. Cruising mainly along the northern shore of the United States, three Canadian privateers—the *Liverpool Packet* (5 guns), *Sir John Sherbrooke* (18 guns), and *Retaliation* (5 guns)—brought some eighty prizes into port. Using privately armed vessels to prey on the enemy's commerce was something that both sides could do.

54 | What was the public response to the outcome of the campaign of 1812?

On both sides of the Atlantic, it was mixed. In the United States, despite the successes at sea, the public could see that the conquest of Canada was going to be more difficult than imagined and that victory was by no means certain. Worse, the defeats in 1812 revealed the sad state of the U.S. Army. "The degraded state in which the military institutions have been retained," concluded the Philadelphia *Aurora*, "comes now upon us with a dismal sentence of retribution."[13] If the Americans were going to win this war, they had to find a way to significantly improve their army.

Not surprisingly, the American failures in 1812 also had an impact on the elections that year. Contesting Madison's bid for re-election was De Witt Clinton, a dissident New York Republican. Clinton won the support of many northern Republicans as well as the Federalists, who decided not to field a candidate of their own. Madison prevailed, but only because he carried Pennsylvania, which was prospering from fat war contracts. The Republicans retained control of both houses of Congress, but the Federalists cut into their majorities.

In Great Britain, the government was embarrassed by the naval losses, and the death of General Brock at Queenston Heights deprived the crown of its best general in North America. Still, the British could take a measure of satisfaction in having fended off the American invasion of Canada. Despite its vulnerability, Canada remained in British hands, and as long as that was the case, the British were winning the war.

55 | Were there any other developments worth noting in 1812?

Yes. "Uncle Sam" made his first appearance. In late December, the Bennington (Vermont) *News-Letter* published a letter from a Federalist complaining about the war. "Now, Mr. Editor," wrote the Federalist, "pray if you can inform me, what single solitary good thing will, or can ac[c]rue to (Uncle Sam) the U.S. for all the expence, marching and countermarching, pain, sickness, death &c. among us?"[14] This is the first known instance of the term "Uncle Sam," a nickname that appeared with increasing frequency during the war. Although on this occasion it referred to the U.S. government, it was also applied to the nation and the army.

CHAPTER THREE

The Second Invasion of Canada

56 | What was American strategy in 1813?

About the same as it was in 1812. With about 30,000 regulars in service, the United States launched another three-pronged attack against Canada. The attack in the Old Northwest again focused on the Detroit River, the attack in the center on the Niagara River, and the attack farther east on Montreal. The United States also continued to wage war against Britain's native allies in the Old Northwest and got involved in a new Indian war with the Creeks in the Old Southwest.

57 | What was British strategy in 1813?

With 20,000 regulars now in service in Canada, the British remained on the defensive. As in 1812, however, they were prepared to exploit any opportunities where the enemy was weak, and they took the offensive in the Old Northwest at the beginning of the campaigning season and on the Niagara River at the end.

58 | Why did the British take the offensive in the Old Northwest?

They knew that the United States was strengthening its position in the region, and they wanted to strike while they could.

They were also under pressure from their Indian allies to mount an offensive. Using Fort Amherstburg as his base, Henry Procter, who was promoted first to brigadier general and then to major general for his part in the British victories at Detroit and Frenchtown, twice led an Anglo-Indian force into Ohio but was unable to duplicate his earlier success. His targets were Fort Meigs (located at the Rapids of the Maumee River in present-day Perrysburg) and Fort Stephenson (in present-day Fremont).

59 | What happened in the first siege of Fort Meigs?

In the spring of 1813, General Procter led 1,000 regulars and militia to the Maumee River, where he was joined by 1,200 Indians under Tecumseh. From May 1 through May 9, the combined force laid siege to Fort Meigs, which was defended by 1,100 American regulars and militia under William Henry Harrison. Fire from Procter's small field guns was ineffective against the fort's interior earthworks, and on May 5, 1,200 militia under Brigadier General Green Clay arrived from Kentucky to relieve Harrison. The Kentucky militia captured some British batteries, but in their enthusiastic pursuit of the enemy they ran into a vicious counterattack that left about half the Americans killed, wounded, or captured. Some forty American prisoners were killed by their Indian captors, and only the intervention of Tecumseh and British Indian agent Matthew Elliott ended the carnage. Ultimately, Procter had to call off the siege because his force was breaking up—his Indian allies were drifting off with what booty they could find, and his militiamen were returning home to plant their crops. Although total American losses in the first siege of Fort Meigs were almost 900 (compared to only 100 for the British), the post remained in American hands.

60 | What happened in the second siege of Fort Meigs?

In July, Procter (now a major general) marched back into Ohio with 500 regulars and militia and a large body of Indians. The invaders tried to lure the Americans out of the fort by staging a sham battle nearby, but General Green Clay, who had replaced Harrison as commander of the fort, knew that no American troops were in the vicinity and refused the bait. For a week, from July 21 through July 28, the invaders laid siege to Fort Meigs, but they were without adequate artillery. Since the fort was unlikely to be taken by storm, Procter had little choice but to lift the siege.

61 | What happened in the Battle of Fort Stephenson?

Unwilling to return home empty-handed, Procter ordered 400 regulars to join a body of Indians in an assault on Fort Stephenson on the Sandusky River. The fort was defended by only 160 Americans under Major George Croghan (pronounced Crawn). Harrison was inclined to abandon the fort, but Croghan convinced him that it could be held, and so Harrison relented.

On August 1, the Anglo-Indian force demanded that Croghan surrender, but he refused. The British opened an artillery bombardment the next day and then, without any help from their Indian friends, tried to take the fort by storm. When the British reached a ditch in front of the fort, they were cut down by Kentucky sharpshooters and a hidden French 6-pounder called "Good Bess." Procter gave up the attack and marched his army back to Canada. The assault on Fort Stephenson had cost him almost a hundred men, while Croghan had sustained only eight casualties. Procter's withdrawal ended the British offensive in the Old Northwest. By then the momentum of the campaign was shifting to the United States because Harrison was preparing his large army for action, and Oliver Hazard Perry's naval squadron was ready to challenge the British for control of Lake Erie.

62 | How did Perry challenge the British on Lake Erie?

By first undertaking an ambitious ship-building program and then by defeating the British in battle. After being given command of American forces on Lake Erie, Perry developed a naval base at Presque Isle (now Erie, Pennsylvania) to build a small squadron of warships that could challenge the British for control of the lake. By August 1813, Perry's squadron, headed by two 20-gun brigs, the *Lawrence* and the *Niagara*, was ready for action. Sailing west to South Bass Island, Perry made Put-in-Bay his base and threatened to shut down the pipeline that kept British regulars and their numerous Indian allies on the Detroit River supplied with food.

Perry's British counterpart, Commander Robert H. Barclay, knew that the American squadron had more firepower (almost 75 percent more), but he had little choice but to challenge Perry in order to keep British supply lines open. On September 10, Barclay sailed from his base at Fort Amherstburg on the Detroit River into the lake to engage Perry. The American officer responded by leading his flagship, the *Lawrence,* into the heart of the British squadron and exchanging deadly broadsides until most of his ship's guns and men were knocked out of action. Instead of surrendering, Perry hauled down his battle flag, which was emblazoned with the words "DON'T GIVE UP THE SHIP," jumped into a boat manned by several seamen, and rowed to *Lawrence*'s sister ship, the *Niagara*, which had not yet engaged the enemy. With a fresh ship and crew, Perry attacked again. This time, assisted by other vessels in his squadron, he battered the damaged and inferior British force into submission.

Having prevailed in the Battle of Lake Erie, Perry now added more luster to his name by sending a simple note to General Har-

This dramatic painting depicts Master Commandant Oliver H. Perry switching ships in the Battle of Lake Erie in 1813. With a new flagship, Perry sailed back into the battle and into history. Note that Perry's battle flag—emblazoned with "DON'T GIVE UP THE SHIP"—is hanging from his hand and draped across the bow of the boat. (Painting by Percy Moran. Library of Congress.)

rison that read: "We have met the enemy and they are ours: Two Ships, two Brigs, one Schooner & one Sloop."[15] This concise message immediately became one of the most celebrated after-action reports in history.

63 | What did Master Commandant Jesse Elliott contribute to Perry's victory?

Very little, and that was to be a source of bitter controversy in later years. Elliott was in charge of the *Niagara* early in the battle, but for reasons that have never been satisfactorily explained, he did not bring his ship up to engage the British. It was only after Perry took command of the *Niagara* that it entered the action.

In the first flush of victory, Perry chose not to question Elliott's actions, but word soon spread that Elliott had not done his duty during the battle, and that precipitated a rancorous debate between the principals and their friends. The controversy continued until Perry's death in 1819 and probably contributed to Captain Stephen Decatur's death the following year in a duel with Captain James Barron (who had been suspended from the Navy for five years for his role in the *Chesapeake* affair in 1807).

64 | What was the impact of Perry's victory?

The British position on the Detroit frontier was now untenable because the commissary had no way of getting food and other supplies to their forces there. General Procter was determined to withdraw eastward, but he did so only over the bitter protests of Tecumseh and his Indian allies and only after promising to make a stand somewhere along the way. Procter moved slowly, and he left the bridges he crossed intact so that his Indian allies could follow him. As a result, Harrison, who had arrived on the Detroit River with 3,000 men, caught up with the retreating Anglo-Indian army about fifty miles east of Detroit.

65 | What was the Battle of the Thames?

With perhaps 500 regulars and 500 Indians, General Procter made his stand. The engagement, fought on October 5, is known as the Battle of the Thames or the Battle of Moraviantown. In the opening minutes of the fighting, Harrison's mounted volunteer militia from Kentucky shouting "Remember the Raisin!" slashed through the two thin British lines, dismounted, and caught them in a crossfire. Within half an hour the British had surrendered. The Indians fought on longer, but when Tecumseh was killed, evidently by Colonel Richard M. Johnson, who was himself wounded four times, the Indians melted away in the wilderness.

Procter managed to escape but was later court-martialed and publicly reprimanded for mismanaging the campaign, and he was never again given a command. The day after the battle Kentucky volunteers, eager to take souvenirs home, stripped and mutilated Tecumseh's swollen body. "I [helped] kill Tecumseh and [helped] *skin him*," a veteran of the campaign recalled many years later, "and brot two pieces of his yellow hide home with me to my mother & sweet harts."[16]

66 | What was the impact of the Battle of the Thames

The Battle of the Thames changed the balance of power in the Old Northwest. The United States regained all that it had lost the year before and even occupied a strip of territory on the Canadian side of the Detroit River. With Tecumseh dead, the native confederacy that he and his brother had forged collapsed, and with the United States now in the ascendant, most of Britain's Indian allies defected and made peace with the young republic. But the British still retained some influence in the region. Their control of Mackinac Island gave them a base from which to supply those Indians who remained loyal. Indians continued to harass American frontier settlements and to skirmish with American forces in the region.

67 | What happened on Lake Ontario in 1813?

Just as Perry challenged Barclay for control on Lake Erie, Captain Isaac Chauncey challenged Commodore James Yeo for com-

BATTLE OF THE THAMES.
5th Oct. 1813.
Respectfully Dedicated to Andrew Jackson Esq. President of the United States

The Battle of the Thames reestablished U.S. dominance in the Old Northwest. This print portrays—with considerable artistic license—Richard M. Johnson and Tecumseh at center stage. (Lithograph by John Dorival. Library of Congress.)

mand of Lake Ontario. Because Ontario lay farther to the east, it was closer to the centers of commerce and population and thus the more important of the two lakes. In what has been dubbed a "shipbuilder's war," both sides poured resources into their respective naval construction programs, the British at Kingston and York and the Americans at Sackets Harbor. Command of the lake see-sawed back and forth as each side put ever larger ships into service. Unlike Barclay on Lake Erie, however, neither commander had a compelling reason to engage the enemy while at a disadvantage. No decisive battle took place on this lake, although Chauncey lost the *Hamilton* and *Scourge,* and Yeo barely escaped capture in the "Burlington Races."

68 | How were *Hamilton* and *Scourge* lost?

In the race to gain naval superiority, the United States drafted some merchant vessels into service that were ill-suited to carry the heavy guns that were subsequently mounted on them. Such was the case with two schooners, the *Hamilton* (carrying 9 guns) and the *Scourge* (mounting 10). The former was an American merchant vessel that had been purchased from its owner and converted into a warship; the latter was seized from the British and refitted as a warship. Both schooners carried far too much weight for their design and were poor sailers in danger of capsizing in rough weather. A seaman on the *Scourge* said that it was widely believed by his mates that "she would prove our coffin."[17] Unfortunately, for many of the crew, his prediction came true.

Early on the morning of August 8, both schooners capsized in a storm and sank. All but sixteen of the hundred men aboard drowned. The two vessels were perfectly preserved on the bottom of the lake, 300 feet beneath the surface, when they were rediscovered in 1973. The U.S. Navy has given title to the schooners to the nearby city of Hamilton, Ontario, so that if the "ghost ships" ever are raised, they will be put on display there.

69 | What were the "Burlington Races"?

On September 28, the opposing squadrons on Lake Ontario cautiously sparred about twelve miles south of York. Yeo's flagship, H.M. Ship *Wolfe* (21 guns), was seriously damaged and fled with the rest of the British squadron toward Burlington Heights at the western end of the lake. Chauncey gave pursuit. Driven by gale force winds, the two squadrons made exceptionally good time in what is usually referred to as the "Burlington Races."

Contrary to local lore, Yeo did not escape by riding the surging surf over a sandbar into what is now Hamilton Harbour. Rather, he anchored his ships outside the bar. Fearing that the strong winds might drive his ships ashore, Chauncey gave up his pursuit, and that ended the engagement.

70 | Why did the United States attack York?

The natural target of the opposing squadrons on the lake was the naval base of the other. But instead of attacking the main British base at Kingston, the United States targeted a secondary base at York (now Toronto), the provincial capital of Upper Canada. Why was York chosen? Mainly because it was an easy target. Kingston was much more strongly defended, and Dearborn and Chauncey overestimated British troop strength there. They therefore decided to attack York instead.

Chauncey ferried some 2,600 army and naval personnel from Sackets Harbor to York, where a successful amphibious landing was made on April 27. The defenders, a motley force of about 1,000 regulars, militia, volunteers, and Indians under General Roger Sheaffe, were forced to withdraw. When Sheaffe ordered the grand magazine blown up, the explosion shook windows at Fort Niagara thirty miles away and killed some 265 Americans who were nearby, including General Zebulon Pike. In all, the United States sustained over 300 casualties, compared to only 200 for the British.

Furious over the carnage done by the explosion, American soldiers burned the provincial parliament and several other public buildings. They also looted the town. In this, they were aided by men they had released from the jail at York and by local opportunists who had come in from the countryside. Dearborn, unwilling to put his life on the line, did not come ashore until after the fighting had ended, and he was slow to stop the rampaging American troops. British officials vigorously protested against these depredations and threatened retaliation.

71 | What was the Battle of Sackets Harbor?

When Captain Chauncey remained at the eastern end of Lake Ontario, the British took advantage of his absence to attack Sackets Harbor. In late May, Yeo ferried 950 men under the overall command of Sir George Prevost but the immediate command of Colonel Edward Baynes to Sackets Harbor for an amphibious landing. When the British landed on May 29, they were met by 1,450 regulars and militia under Brigadier General Jacob Brown of the New York militia. While the outcome of the ensuing engagement was still in doubt, an American midshipman, believing that all was lost, put the naval yard and its stores to the torch. Although the conflagration was put out by a hastily organized fire brigade, the British, believing that the destruction of the yard had been accomplished, withdrew. The British lost 250 men in the Battle of Sackets Harbor, the Americans around 300. Brown was rewarded with a commission as brigadier general in the regular army.

72 | What was the Battle of Fort George?

The capture of York was but a preliminary to the main operation on the Niagara front. The United States planned to capture Fort George, roll back Britain's position on the Niagara River, and destroy the British army defending the Niagara Peninsula. The campaign began in a promising manner with the capture of Fort George but ended with British successes all along the front.

After bombarding Fort George for two days, Captain Chauncey on May 27 ferried 4,000 men to the shore near the British fort.

The invading force was nominally under the command of Major General Morgan Lewis, but the attack had been planned and carried out by Colonel Winfield Scott. General John Vincent met the invaders on the shoreline but had only about 1,400 British regulars, militia, and Indians under his command. Overwhelmed by artillery fire from the American shore and from Chauncey's ships as well as by Scott's assault force, Vincent fell back to Fort George. He then fled west and ordered all British troops stationed along the Niagara River to follow him. American losses in the assault on Fort George were 140, while British losses were 350.

It could have been worse for the British because Winfield Scott followed their retreat. Had he caught up with them, he might have destroyed the entire British force, but he was ordered to give up the pursuit by the excessively cautious Lewis. Vincent made it safely to Burlington Heights with some 1,600 troops and was still in a position to challenge the American force that now occupied Fort George.

73 | What happened in the Battle of Stoney Creek?

To challenge Vincent's army, Brigadier General William Winder marched west from Fort George with 1,400 men. He was soon joined by another 1,100 men under Brigadier General John Chandler. As the senior brigadier, Chandler assumed command. After skirmishing with the British on June 5, Chandler ordered his men to make camp. Although he expected to be attacked, he did not deploy his force to the best advantage, and only about 1,300 men were on the ground that would be contested in the battle that ensued.

Meanwhile, Lieutenant Colonel John Harvey had persuaded General Vincent to let him hazard a risky night attack with around 750 men. In the confused fighting that followed, both sides suffered casualties from friendly fire. Harvey was very nearly defeated, but the tide turned when his men overran three American artillery pieces and both American generals were captured after blundering into British units. By the time the fighting had ended, the British had lost 215 men, the Americans 170.

Although the battle was nominally a draw, the Americans had failed to destroy Vincent's army. In addition, they had lost two generals and precipitously departed the next day without burying their dead or carrying off their equipment and supplies.

74 | What happened in the Battle of Beaver Dams?

On June 23, Lieutenant Colonel Charles Boerstler marched 600 men from Fort George to Queenston and from there headed for Beaver Dams in the hope of destroying a small British outpost of some fifty men under Lieutenant James FitzGibbon that had been harassing Americans who ventured from the fort. But FitzGibbon was not as vulnerable as Boerstler thought. Some 450 Indians were camped nearby, and FitzGibbon had been warned that an American attack was imminent, first by a local resident, Laura Secord, who trekked twenty miles through the wilderness in the dead of night to deliver the warning, and then by Indian scouts who had monitored Boerstler's progress.

On June 24, before Boerstler made it to the British outpost, he was ambushed by some 400 Indians. FitzGibbon then arrived on the scene and by greatly exaggerating the size of his command and playing on Boerstler's fears of an Indian massacre persuaded the American officer to surrender his entire force.

75 | What was the impact of the American defeats at Stoney Creek and Beaver Dams?

The American failure in these battles put an end to offensive operations from Fort George. The twin defeats also put an end to

Dearborn's timid and inept leadership on the Niagara front. His critics became more numerous and more vocal, and the administration responded by transferring him, ostensibly for health reasons, to New York City, where he could not further damage the war effort.

Dearborn was succeeded at Fort George by a New York militia officer, Brigadier General George McClure, who lacked command experience and was unpopular with his men. McClure's army shrank as regulars were ordered east for a major operation against Montreal, and he was unable to persuade unpaid militiamen, whose term of service was up, to remain. Convinced that the defense of the fort had become impossible, McClure on December 10 ordered it evacuated and nearby Newark (now the beautiful resort town of Niagara-on-the-Lake) burned. The residents of the village were left without housing in the dead of winter as 150 buildings went up in flames.

76 | Why was Newark burned?

Largely because of General McClure's bad judgment. The War Department had ordered McClure to burn the town only if it was necessary to protect the fort. Once McClure decided to abandon the fort, there was no reason to burn Newark. McClure claimed the destruction of the town was necessary to deny British troops housing, but there was plenty of other housing available in the area, and the British could also use the fort. Despite McClure's order to destroy the post, those Americans assigned to the task fled before the job was done because a British force approached. The destruction of Newark was not only needless, it invited retaliation.

77 | How did the British respond to the destruction of Newark?

They were furious and determined to retaliate. Lieutenant General Gordon Drummond was now in command of British forces on the Niagara, and he launched a campaign to capture Fort Niagara and destroy American settlements all along the river.

Late on December 18, under cover of darkness, Drummond dispatched Colonel John Murray and 550 men across the river to the outskirts of Fort Niagara. After securing the sign and countersign from a frightened picket they had surprised, the British slipped into the American fort after midnight. The fort's commander, Captain Nathan Leonard, a notorious drunkard, was sleeping in his home three miles away. He had taken no precautions against an attack, and consequently the Americans were caught by surprise, mostly asleep. The British offered no quarter to those who resisted and inflicted eighty casualties, mainly with the bayonet. They captured another 350 men, including Leonard when he returned to his post the next morning, and bagged a huge quantity of war materiel. Their own losses were only about a dozen.

After capturing Fort Niagara, a British force commanded by General Phineas Riall burned the nearby villages of Lewiston, Youngstown, and Manchester. The Indians who accompanied them left a ghastly scene. "Our neighbors were seen lying dead in the fields and roads," reported an American who later visited Lewiston, "some horribly cut and mangled with tomahawks, others eaten by the hogs."[18]

Nor were the British done. They returned on December 30 and burned Buffalo and Black Rock at the southern end of the river. By that time General McClure was so reviled that he fled the front, and the British had no trouble routing the militia summoned by his successor, Brigadier General Amos Hall. The only stiff resistance the British met at Buffalo was from a group of renegades from Canada led by the notorious Joseph Willcocks.

A campaign that had opened with such promise with the capture of Fort George six months earlier ended with the British in control of both forts at the mouth of the Niagara and the American side of the river in flames. "The whole frontier from Lake Ontario to Lake Erie," lamented Governor Daniel D. Tompkins of New York, "is depopulated & the buildings & improvements, with a few exceptions, destroyed."[19]

78 | Who was Joseph Willcocks and why was he so notorious?

Joseph Willcocks was a Canadian traitor who was probably the most hated person in Canada. Although he liked to portray himself as a defender of freedom, he was mainly an opportunist who could be ruthless and vindictive. Willcocks worked closely with British officials to defend Canada early in the war, but after the United States captured Fort George, he led seventy-five men across the border and offered his services to the United States. American officials gave him a military commission, first as a major then as a lieutenant colonel, and Willcocks organized his men into a unit called the Canadian Volunteers.

With intimate knowledge of the geography and the people on the Canadian side of the river, Willcocks and his Volunteers were a valuable source of intelligence on the Niagara front. They could also be counted on in the heat of battle because, to them, surrender or capture meant hanging. But Willcocks had a darker side. He used the war as an excuse to settle old scores, and his predatory raids into Canada were little more than a pretext to burn private property and seize civilians on his target list. Willcocks and the Volunteers had a hand in the destruction of Newark as well as several other towns in Upper Canada. Willcocks probably hoped to terrorize the local population into submission, but his brutal form of warfare had the opposite effect, increasing support for the British government and promoting Canadian patriotism.

When Willcocks was killed in a skirmish near Fort Erie in September 1814, his followers melted away. Since they could not return to Canada, they remained in the United States after the war, and the government ultimately rewarded them with land grants.

79 | What was the American strategy for capturing Montreal?

The plan was to assault the city from two directions. Major General James Wilkinson would sail with one army, about 7,300 men, from Sackets Harbor to the mouth of the St. Lawrence, then go downriver toward Montreal. A second army, 6,000 strong and headed by Major General Wade Hampton, would depart from Plattsburgh and head north toward Montreal. The combined force was the largest sent against any Canadian target during the war, but from the beginning this double-barreled operation was beset by problems.

The campaign did not get under way until October, far too late in the season. Neither commander showed much ability or much enthusiasm. Wilkinson, a one-time Spanish spy with an appetite for booty and a penchant for intrigue, had a reputation for putting his own interests above those of his troops or his country. He had so little confidence in the plan of operations that he told the secretary of war that if things went awry he might have to surrender. Wilkinson was also beset by dysentery during most of the campaign, and the opiates he took to dull his intestinal pain clouded his faculties. Hampton was hardly more effective. The haughty South Carolinian so despised Wilkinson that he refused to take orders from him. Montreal in any case would be a tough nut to crack. By the fall of 1813, the British had amassed 6,000 troops for the defense of the city.

As it happened, neither American army got close to Montreal. Hampton was stopped at the Battle of Châteauguay on October 26, and Wilkinson was beaten in the Battle of Crysler's Farm on November 11. Since neither commander had much faith in the plan of operations, these defeats ended the campaign, and each army limped back to the United States and into winter quarters.

80 | What happened in the Battle of Châteauguay?

On September 19, Hampton sailed from Plattsburgh to the northern end of Lake Champlain. There he landed his force, marched into Canada, and fought his way into Odelltown. But facing more resistance and a lack of water, he veered southwest to Four Corners (present-day Chateaugay, New York), where he made camp and spent several weeks improving his supply route and waiting for further orders. He finally received orders to proceed with the campaign in mid-October. By then, the weather had turned cold and rainy, and since Hampton's militia would not leave the United States, he entered Canada with only 3,800 men, most of whom were raw troops.

On October 25, Hampton ran into resistance from some 1,950 men, mostly French Canadians, under the command of Lieutenant Colonel Charles de Salaberry. The next day, Hampton advanced on both sides of the Châteauguay River, but after six or eight hours of fitful fighting, he concluded that the operation was unlikely to succeed and ordered a withdrawal to Plattsburgh. Casualties on both sides were light, maybe fifty Americans and twenty-five French Canadians, but it was a clear British victory against a much larger American force.

81 | What happened in the Battle of Crysler's Farm?

Wilkinson was even slower to get his part of the campaign under way. He did not sail from Sackets Harbor until mid-October. Contrary winds and the loss of supplies further delayed his progress so that the bulk of his army did not reach the St. Lawrence River until early November. Although he had to contend with harassing British fire from the shore, Wilkinson pressed ahead and reached Long Sault (now called the International Rapids). General Jacob Brown cleared the north shore and advanced ahead to Cornwall, but Wilkinson soon discovered that another British force of about 1,200 regulars, militia, and Mohawk Indians under the command of Lieutenant Colonel Joseph W. Morrison threatened his rear. Morrison's army established a strong defensive position on the north side of the St. Lawrence at Crysler's Farm.

Since Wilkinson was too ill to take part in any battle, he sent Brigadier General John P. Boyd, a veteran of Tippecanoe, with 3,000 men to dislodge Morrison's force on November 11. Boyd provided little guidance to his men during the engagement and attacked piecemeal, which allowed the British to defeat his larger force in detail. Boyd finally ordered a retreat, leaving many of his wounded on the field. British surgeons tended to the American wounded, but they were now prisoners of war. The United States had lost 400 men in the battle, the British a little over 200. Among the American dead was promising forty-five-year-old officer, Leonard Covington, who had just been promoted to brigadier general of the U.S. Army.

The day after this defeat, Wilkinson moved his army downriver to the vicinity of Cornwall. Here he learned that Hampton had called off his part of the campaign. That was all the excuse Wilkinson needed to end his own operation. He ordered his army into winter quarters at French Mills (now Fort Covington), New York, where harsh winter conditions took a heavy toll on the demoralized American troops. Wilkinson's defeat effectively marked the end of American operations on the northern border in 1813.

82 | What caused the Creek War in the Old Southwest?

It grew broadly out of American land hunger but more immediately out of a civil war within the Creek confederacy. Occupying most of present-day Alabama, the Creeks were loosely allied to neighboring tribes in a confederation. Although the tribe included many mixed-bloods who embraced white ways, there was a militant band of young men—known as Red Sticks because they painted their war clubs red—who rejected white civilization and were determined to protect their lands from further encroachments. When Tecumseh visited the Creeks in 1811, he found the Red Sticks receptive to his message of resistance.

Emboldened by the Anglo-Indian victories in the Old Northwest in 1812 and by promises of support from Spanish officials in Florida, a group of Red Sticks visited Tecumseh and took part in the Battle of Frenchtown and the River Raisin Massacre in early 1813. On their way home, they raided an American settlement in Kentucky. To keep peace with the Americans, the older Creek leaders ordered the perpetrators of the raid killed. This led to a civil war, and when the Red Sticks prevailed, most of the old leaders had to take refuge with the American Indian agent.

83 | What was the Battle of Burnt Corn?

In July 1813 a group of Red Sticks visited Pensacola in Spanish Florida to trade for European goods. On July 27, while en route home, they were attacked by 180 Mississippi militia in a skirmish known as the Battle of Burnt Corn. The Americans made off with most of the Spanish goods, but because they were driven off the field by a much smaller Indian force, the Red Sticks were emboldened. The Battle of Burnt Corn transformed what had been a civil war among Creeks into a larger war with the United States.

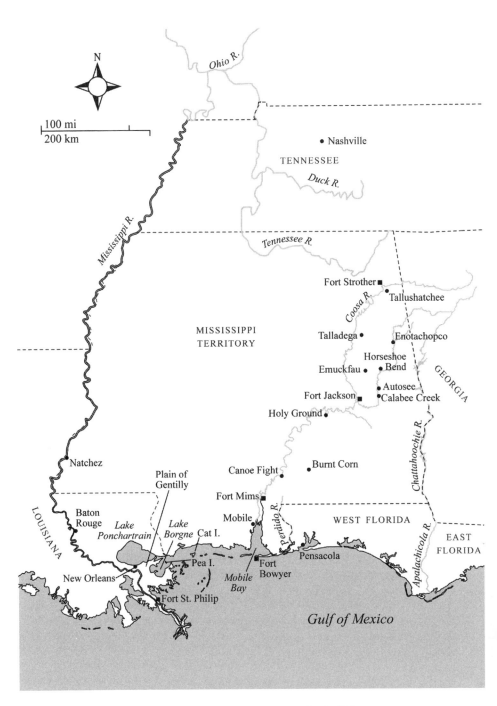

The War in the Southwest and on the Gulf Coast.

84 | What was the Fort Mims Massacre?

A month after Burnt Corn, the Red Sticks retaliated by attacking Fort Mims, a stockade forty miles north of Mobile. Close to 200 American civilians had taken refuge in the fort, which was defended by 120 militia under a regular army officer, Major Daniel Beasley, who took his duties lightly and ignored reports that Indians were seen in the vicinity. On August 30, the Red Sticks caught the defenders by surprise and after some hard fighting overwhelmed them. Most of the Americans were killed, although a few whites escaped into the woods and the Indians carried off some of the black slaves. But the defenders sold their lives dearly. At least 100 Indians were killed and many more wounded. Contemporary reports exaggerated the number of Americans killed, and settlers in the Old Southwest called for revenge.

85 | How did the United States respond to the Fort Mims Massacre?

In the late fall of 1813, Andrew Jackson, a major general in the Tennessee militia, led a punitive expedition into Indian country. Over the next four months, Jackson had to contend with a host of problems: obstreperous militia and volunteers, inadequate supplies, lukewarm support from state and federal officials, and the lack of enough regular troops to carry on an extended campaign. But in the end, "Old Hickory" overcame those obstacles and defeated the Red Sticks.

86 | How did Jackson maintain discipline in his army?

With a heavy hand. During his campaign against the Creeks, Jackson faced persistent problems, particularly from militia and volunteers who had their own ideas about camp discipline and how long their service ought to last. On occasion, Jackson had to threaten to use militia against volunteers or volunteers against militia to keep his motley army intact, and twice he leveled his own musket against men threatening to go home.

On two occasions Jackson resorted to the severest form of military punishment to maintain order. In February 1814, when eighteen-year-old Private John Woods of the Tennessee militia refused to obey an order, Jackson ordered him court-martialed. Woods was convicted of disobedience and mutiny and on March 14 was shot by a firing squad, the first execution of a citizen soldier since the Revolution. The sanguinary lesson was not lost on the rest of Jackson's men. According to one of Jackson's aides, "a strict obedience afterwards characterized the army."[20]

Later that year Jackson took an equally hard line against a group of Tennessee militia who had gone home because they were convinced that their term of service was up. When the men later returned to camp, Jackson ordered them court-martialed. The court found them guilty. Although most were sentenced to forfeit part of their pay, make up lost time, and then be drummed out of camp with their heads partly shaved, the ringleaders—a sergeant and five privates—were ordered to be shot by a firing squad. On February 21, 1815, this order was carried out. Even though rumors of peace were circulating and the war was in fact over, Jackson showed no mercy.

Although Jackson's enemies never let the public forget his harsh brand of military justice, it had a sobering effect on his troops and helped him maintain discipline and order. Jackson was an effective leader for a variety of reasons, not the least of which was that his men feared him more than they feared the enemy.

87 | What was the Battle of Horseshoe Bend?

It was the climax of the Creek War. In late 1813 Jackson had won a series of preliminary victories that weakened the Red Sticks, who now referred to the American general as "Sharp Knife" or "Pointed Arrow." By February 1814, Jackson had built a large enough army—about 4,000 men—and had stockpiled enough food and other supplies to challenge the Red Sticks deep in their own country. Learning from friendly Indians that the Red Sticks had fortified a peninsula called Horseshoe Bend on the Tallapoosa River (near present-day Daviston, Alabama), Jackson marched to the scene with 3,000 men and on March 27 launched a well-planned attack. While friendly Indians swam across the river and made off with the Red Sticks' canoes so that they could not escape by water, Jackson opened up with his field artillery. When the artillery proved ineffective, Jackson ordered a frontal assault with one force while a second used the Red Sticks' canoes to re-cross the river and attack from the rear.

Once the Red Sticks' defenses were breached, they were overwhelmed, and the battle turned into a massacre. Most of the Creeks refused to surrender, and those who tried to escape were shot down. Even Jackson admitted that the *"carnage was dreadfull."*[21] Close to 800 Creeks perished in the battle, while Jackson's own casualties numbered only about 200.

88 | Who was William Weatherford and what was his role in the Creek War?

An affluent Scottish-Creek mixed-blood who was also known as Red Eagle, William Weatherford was a Red Stick leader who took part in the Fort Mims Massacre and most of the battles in the Creek War. Although apparently not at Horseshoe Bend, Weatherford chose to surrender to Jackson after the battle rather than flee to Florida with other Red Stick survivors. Jackson spared Weatherford's life and used him to bring other Creeks to the peace table at Fort Jackson. After the war, Weatherford rebuilt his fortune in

Alabama, and by the time he died in 1824, he was a successful plantation owner who had amassed a sizeable estate.

89 | What was the Treaty of Fort Jackson?

It was the draconian peace that Jackson imposed on all Creeks, friend and foe alike, on August 9, 1814, at Fort Jackson (located near present-day Wetumpka, Alabama). Even though many Creeks had fought side-by-side with Jackson's men against the Red Sticks, he insisted that all tribal leaders sign the treaty, which stripped the Indians of an astonishing twenty million acres of land, fully half their territory. Such a land grab left friendly Indians and officials in Washington aghast, but Americans living in the West considered it a fitting end to the Creek War and welcomed the boost it gave to national expansion.

90 | How did the British bring their naval power to bear in 1813?

Despite commitments all over the globe, the British were able to shift enough warships to America to establish a blockade of the Atlantic seaboard and to conduct predatory raids along the coast. Admiral Sir John Borlase Warren had initiated an unofficial blockade of the American coast from Charleston, South Carolina, to Spanish Florida in the fall of 1812, and in the first half of 1813 he gradually extended this blockade to the ports and harbors in other middle and southern states. At the same time he detailed Rear Admiral Sir George Cockburn (pronounced Co-burn) to conduct raids in the Chesapeake. Warren hoped that Cockburn's raids would force the United States to shift regulars away from the Canadian frontier. Although the raids failed to achieve this aim, they certainly showed Americans the sharp edge of British naval power.

91 | Why wasn't New England blockaded?

The number of warships the Admiralty was willing to deploy to America was limited, and British officials preferred to devote those resources to states dominated by Republicans who supported the war. Exempting New England from the blockade was a way of rewarding anti-war Federalists who controlled the region. In addition, the British army in Canada was dependent on food imported from New York and New England, and British officials did not want to disrupt this trade. British armies in the Spanish Peninsula were also dependent on American grain, which was usually shipped to them in ships owned by New England merchants that were sailing under British licenses.

92 | How effective was the British blockade?

The results were mixed. The U.S. coast was so long and irregular that a complete blockade was impossible. In addition, the British had only a limited number of ships at their disposal to do the job, and those ships could be blown off station by a storm. American warships and privateers had opportunities to make a run for open waters.

The impact of the British blockade on the American economy, on the other hand, was staggering. It was already dangerous for merchants to send their ships to foreign ports, and with the Royal Navy on the coast, that danger increased. Marine insurance rates soared to 50 percent or more. This meant that a merchant who wanted to engage in trade had to shell out half the value of the ship and cargo to insure any voyage. The coastal trade was also disrupted, and moving freight overland was difficult and expensive. The roads were crude, and heavy traffic coupled with the assault of the elements made them worse. One contemporary complained that it took thirty-eight hours to travel fifty miles from Alexandria

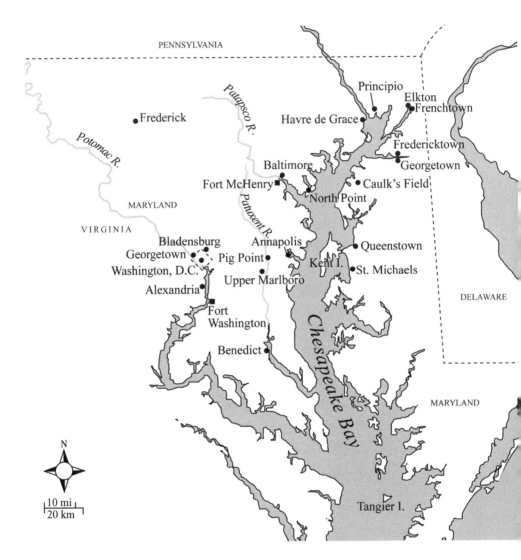

The war in the Chesapeake Bay.

to Fredericksburg, Virginia, a trip that normally could be done in half the time, and another said that so many wagons were carrying goods between Trenton, New Jersey, and New York City that "the road is literally cut hub deep."[22]

With trade sharply curtailed, gluts and shortages appeared everywhere. Rice, which cost $3 a hundredweight in Charleston or

Savannah, sold for $9 in New York and $12 in Boston. Likewise, flour that went for $4.50 a barrel in Richmond commanded $8.50 in New York and $12 in Boston.

The British blockade also took a toll on public finance. Despite a sizeable tax increase, federal revenue, which came mostly from taxes on trade, fell below peacetime levels, and this at a time when the cost of the war was soaring. The growing deficit suggested that if the war lasted much longer, a bankrupt government might have to resort to paper money or some other dubious expedient.

93 | Why did the British target the Chesapeake?

It was well settled and prosperous, and it offered the Royal Navy easy access and a relatively safe anchorage. Under the command of Rear Admiral Cockburn, the British plundered at will in 1813. Cockburn had a talent for amphibious operations, and he considered fair game all public property and merchant vessels and any commodities produced for export. If the British raiding parties, mostly Royal seamen and marines, met with resistance from any town, they considered it a military garrison subject to destruction. Some towns escaped damage by capitulating. Others were spared because militia called out arrived too late to offer any resistance. Those towns that put up a fight occasionally succeeded, but untrained militia units were usually no match for battle-hardened professionals backed by naval power.

Maryland bore the brunt of these attacks. In the space of a week in the spring of 1813, Cockburn's men torched Frenchtown, Havre de Grace, Fredericktown, and Georgetown and compelled Charlestown to surrender. They also destroyed the Principio Ironworks in Cecil County. Although the British usually had their way, occasionally they were rebuffed. They were repulsed at Fort Defiance, which protected Elkton, and when they returned in August a pair of attacks on St. Michaels failed, as did an attack on Queenstown.

94 | What was the Battle of Craney Island?

The British also targeted sites in Virginia, and in June 1813 local forces mounted a successful defense of Norfolk. The British decided to attack Norfolk because the American frigate *Constellation* had taken refuge there and it was home to the Gosport Naval Yard. The assault force, some 2,400 men, included two Independent Companies of Foreigners that consisted of French deserters and prisoners of war who were impossible to control, in part because their French officers were stealing their pay. In charge of the defense of Norfolk was a militia officer, Brigadier General Robert B. Taylor, who had only 800 soldiers, sailors, and Marines at his disposal. Taylor fortified Craney Island, which commanded the approaches, and Captain John Cassin of the Gosport Naval Yard brought up a squadron of gunboats that blocked access to the harbor should the British get past Craney Island.

The British launched a land and water attack on June 22. Both wings of the attack came under heavy artillery fire and ran into natural obstacles that forced them to retreat. The land force could not ford the deep water that separated the island from the mainland, and the British boats became mired in mud far from their target and had to be abandoned. Casualties were not heavy. The British lost twenty killed and wounded but another sixty-two, mostly Frenchmen who had deserted, were missing. The United States reported no casualties in the engagement. The French soldiers, claiming that some of their men had been massacred after their boats ran aground, were determined to avenge these losses.

95 | What happened in the British raid on Hampton?

On June 26, just four days after the defeat at Craney Island, a large British force, again around 2,400 men, attacked Hampton, Virginia. The militia offered stout resistance before giving way and lost only thirty men compared to eighty British casualties. The French soldiers now ran amok, attacking the civilian population. "Every horror was committed with impunity," a British officer conceded, "rape, murder, pillage: and not a man was punished!"[23] The Independent Foreigners were ordered to Halifax, where they remained unruly until their units were shipped to Europe and disbanded. The Hampton atrocities were not soon forgotten. To Americans living in the Chesapeake, the town name became a byword for the British way of war.

96 | Were there any naval engagements in 1813?

Yes, but fewer than in 1812 because the British blockade made it harder for American warships to get to sea. Like the *Constellation* at Norfolk, most were bottled up in port. Even those U.S. ships that got free were less likely to find British warships alone because, after their losses in 1812, Admiralty officials had ordered their frigates to sail in squadrons and to avoid single-ship duels with the heavy American frigates. Of those that did take place, the most significant engagement pitted the U.S. Frigate *Chesapeake* against the British ship *Shannon* off the coast of Massachusetts and the U.S. Frigate *Essex* against two British warships in Chile's territorial waters in the Pacific.

97 | What happened in the duel between the *Chesapeake* and the *Shannon?*

Unlike most other British naval commanders, Captain Philip Broke (pronounced Brook) insisted that the crew of H.M. Ship *Shannon*, which mounted 52 guns, engage in frequent gunnery practice with live ammunition. Broke even fitted his ship with ad-

This dramatic print shows sailors from the Shannon *boarding the U.S. Frigate* Chesapeake. *Despite the pleas of her mortally wounded commander, the* Chesapeake *surrendered. (Drawing by Henry Reuterdahl. A. T. Mahan,* Sea Power and its Relations to the War of 1812.*)*

vanced aiming devices. While off the American coast not far from Boston, he sent his sister ships away and delivered a challenge to Captain James Lawrence, who had just assumed command of the *Chesapeake* (carrying 50 guns), which was fitting out in Boston. Lawrence sailed before the challenge arrived, but he needed no prodding to engage the British ship. In the ensuing contest on June 1, the first fire of the *Shannon* took a heavy toll, particularly on the American officers, and by boarding, the British quickly overwhelmed the American crew and compelled the *Chesapeake* to strike its colors.

The number of casualties—228 killed and wounded on the two ships—made this the bloodiest naval duel of the war. Among the victims was Captain Lawrence, who sustained a mortal wound but repeatedly encouraged his officers with words like "Don't give up the ship!" or similar expressions. Lawrence survived for another three days, but by then the British were sailing the *Chesapeake* to Halifax as a prize of war. Lawrence received a hero's funeral in New York City that was reportedly attended by 50,000 people. He was the only commanding officer to be so honored after losing a battle.

The secretary of the navy named Oliver H. Perry's flagship on Lake Erie after Lawrence, and Perry paid further tribute to the fallen hero by flying a banner emblazoned with the words "DON'T GIVE UP THE SHIP." Perry's victory on the lake immortalized Lawrence's words, and the U.S. Navy subsequently adopted the phrase as its motto.

As for Broke, he was treated as a great hero in Britain for having restored the reputation of the Royal Navy against the upstarts across the Atlantic. News of his victory was greeted with shouts of joy in Parliament, and he was showered with gifts and honors, including a key to the city of London. "Captain Broke and his crew," concluded the London *Morning Chronicle*, "have vindicated the character of the British Navy."[24] Since this was the only naval duel that involved frigates of equal firepower, defenders of the Royal Navy argued with some justice that it offset all the losses of the previous year.

98 | Why did the cruise of the *Essex* become famous?

The U.S. Frigate *Essex*, which in 1800 had been the first U.S. warship to venture into the Indian Ocean, became the first to cruise the waters of the Pacific in 1813. Overloaded with 46 guns (mostly carronades) and commanded by Captain David Porter, the American ship sailed around Cape Horn and targeted British whaling vessels before the Royal Navy dispatched a small squadron to track it down. At Valparaiso, H.M. Ship *Phoebe*, carrying 46 or 53 guns and commanded by Captain James Hillyar, and H.M. Sloop *Cher-*

ub, mounting 26 guns and commanded by Captain Thomas Tucker, caught up with Porter.

The opposing ships waited uneasily in Chilean waters until March 28, 1814, when Porter made a run for the open sea. The *Essex* lost its topmast in a sudden squall, and although Porter's ship was still in Chilean waters, the two British ships moved in for the kill. After a bloody engagement they compelled Porter to surrender.

After the battle, each side accused the other of bad faith. The British claimed that Porter had connived in the escape of his crew after striking his colors, and the Americans accused the British of continuing to fire after they had surrendered. Rather than bad faith on either side, the opposing perceptions were probably just a by-product of the fog of war. The black powder used in battles of this era generated so much smoke that sometimes it was impossible to know with any certainty what was happening.

99 | Was there any privateering in 1813?

Yes, but far less than in 1812. The British blockade made it more difficult for American privateers to get to sea, and because British merchantmen were required to sail in convoy on the high seas, those privateers that managed to get free found fewer targets. British merchants, whether in the home islands or in Canada, also outfitted fewer privateers because the war had driven most American merchantmen from the seas.

In spite of the obstacles, several American privateers enjoyed successful cruises, especially in waters around the British Isles, where British merchant ships were numerous and were not required to sail in convoy. The *True-Blooded Yankee* (16 guns), fitted out by an American in Paris, cruised with impunity in the British Isles for thirty-seven days, taking twenty-seven prizes, burning seven vessels in a Scottish harbor, and occupying an Irish island for six days. "She outsailed everything," remarked a British naval officer; "not one of our cruisers could touch her."[25] The *Scourge* (15 guns) and *Rattlesnake* (16 guns) also did well, taking twenty-three prizes in the North Sea that were condemned in Norwegian ports. The *Scourge* made a second successful cruise in British waters and continued to take prizes as she worked her way home.

100 | What was the public response to the outcome of the campaign of 1813?

Americans were pleased with the progress in the West, particularly the death of Tecumseh, the disintegration of his confederacy, and the nation's ascendancy there. But this theater of operations was too remote to significantly affect the course of the war, and on the more important fronts to the east there was little but defeat and humiliation. After two years of campaigning, the United States found itself no closer to conquering Canada or to winning the war.

Moreover, the death and destruction that the British visited upon the Niagara and the Chesapeake brought the war home to Americans. That was especially true in the Chesapeake, which was a major center of population, wealth, and trade for the young and growing republic. The British campaign there seemed punitive in nature, designed to punish civilians, encourage slaves to run away, and enrich British soldiers and sailors with loot. *Niles' Register* dubbed Admiral Warren the "spoiler of the Chesapeake" and his troops "water-*Winnebagoes*," a reference to the militant western tribe known for its ferocity. Cockburn came in for even more abuse. "The wantonness of his barbarities," said *Niles*, "have gibbetted him on infamy."[26]

The British, on the other hand, might rue the loss of Tecumseh and the Old Northwest, but they could take satisfaction in having preserved Canada for another year. They had reestablished their ascendancy on the Niagara, beaten back an assault that had targeted Montreal, and maintained a formidable naval presence on Lake Ontario. The preservation of Canada meant that after two years of campaigning the British were still winning the war.

CHAPTER FOUR

The British Counterstrike

101 | Did the character of the war change in 1814?

Yes, greatly. The United States found itself mainly on the defensive. This was a direct result of developments in Europe. In the summer of 1812, Napoleon had invaded Russia and lost a large army there. After scrambling to rebuild his forces, the French emperor was defeated again, this time in October 1813 in the Battle of Leipzig (also known as the Battle of the Nations) in modern-day Germany. At the same time, the Duke of Wellington was waging a successful campaign against French armies in the Spanish Peninsula and moving ever closer to the French border. Napoleon's position steadily deteriorated, and on March 31, 1814, Britain's continental allies marched into Paris. A week later Napoleon abdicated and was subsequently sent into exile on the Mediterranean island of Elba. For the first time in more than a decade, there was peace in Europe.

After Leipzig, with the tide in Europe running in their favor, the British began cautiously shifting forces to North America. After Napoleon's abdication the following spring, this redeployment picked up steam. By the spring of 1814, the British had 30,000 troops in North America, and a lot more were on the way. Largely because of enhanced pay and growing enlistment bounties, the United States by this time could muster 40,000 men, but most lacked the training, discipline, and combat experience of their British counterparts. With the British beefing up their military and naval power in America, momentum was turning against the United States.

102 | What was American strategy in 1814?

The United States continued to dominate the Old Northwest and hoped to consolidate its position there by retaking Mackinac. It also planned a major offensive on the Niagara River to drive the British from this peninsula. Everywhere else, the young republic was forced on the defensive and could hope only to defeat the British forces that raided or invaded U.S. territory.

103 | What was British strategy in 1814?

For the first time in the war, the British were able to take the offensive. Although they considered a campaign in the Old Northwest to retake control of occupied Upper Canada and drive Americans from the Detroit frontier, the region was so remote and so difficult to supply without controlling Lake Erie that they had to settle for remaining on the defensive there as well as on the Niagara front. Farther east, they planned offensives in upper New York, on the eastern seaboard, and on the Gulf Coast. Their aim was to seize American territory that might be used as a bargaining chip in peace negotiations and to bring the war home to Americans.

104 | Was the United States able to consolidate its hold on the Old Northwest?

No. Americans were defeated at Mackinac and even lost control of Lake Huron, despite having undisputed command of Lake Erie, which provided ready access to Lake Huron via the Detroit River, Lake St. Clair, and the St. Clair River.

On July 3, Lieutenant Colonel George Croghan, who had orchestrated the defense of Fort Stephenson the previous year, departed from Detroit with 700 regulars and volunteer militia aboard a squadron of U.S. warships commanded by Captain Arthur Sinclair, who had succeeded Captain Perry as the ranking U.S. naval officer on the western lakes. Slowed by contrary winds and shallow water, the squadron made its way into Lake Huron and then sailed north, where it destroyed an unoccupied British fort on St. Joseph Island and looted a North West Company post at Sault Ste. Marie.

Reaching Mackinac on July 26, the Americans discovered that Lieutenant Colonel Robert McDouall, who had about 450 men at his disposal, had significantly upgraded the island's defenses. Sinclair could not elevate his naval artillery enough to hit the two British forts, and Croghan considered them too strong to be taken by storm. Hence, he decided to establish a base on the western side of the island from which he could harass the British and their Indian allies.

The position Croghan chose for his base lay next to a forest, and McDouall was waiting there in the underbrush with a force of regulars, militia, and Indians. Croghan came under fire after he landed on August 4, and when he was unable to dislodge the enemy with a counterattack, he decided to call off the entire campaign. Croghan had never shown much enthusiasm for the assault on Mackinac and was unwilling to continue after he lost several key officers. The Americans had sustained about seventy-five casualties in the battle for Fort Mackinac; the British and their Indian allies perhaps a dozen. The American withdrawal meant that this important post remained in British hands for the rest of the war.

105 | How did the United States lose control of Lake Huron?

Shortly after abandoning the assault on Mackinac, Sinclair

sailed to the Nottawasaga River on Georgian Bay to destroy Britain's lone warship on Lake Huron, H.M. Schooner *Nancy*, a supply ship carrying three guns and commanded by Lieutenant Miller Worsley of the Royal Navy. Sinclair accomplished his mission in the Battle of Nottawasaga on August 14, then sailed back to Lake Erie, leaving two schooners, the *Tigress* (1 gun) and the *Scorpion* (2 guns), to maintain American command of Lake Huron.

Having escaped with most of his men into the wilderness when the *Nancy* was destroyed, Worsley returned to the lake and, using several small boats, made a heroic six-day, 380-mile voyage with his small force to Fort Mackinac, where he secured additional men. Then on the night of September 3, he surprised the *Tigress* and after a brief but furious fire fight gained control of the schooner. Three days later, with the *Tigress* still flying the American flag, he surprised and took the *Scorpion*. In less than seventy-two hours, Worsley had retaken control of Lake Huron. This meant that the British could use the lake to resupply their troops at Fort Mackinac, support their fur traders, and solidify their influence over their remaining Indian allies in the Old Northwest.

106 | Were there other military actions in the region?

Yes, there were. The retention of Mackinac enabled the British to retain a fort at Prairie du Chien, which almost surely would have fallen if Mackinac had been lost. This gave the British two bases in American territory. Britain's Indian allies made good use of these bases to launch raids against American settlements in Illinois, Iowa, and Missouri.

The Americans, however, could mount raids of their own because they controlled Lake Erie and had a strong position on the Detroit River. On May 14 Colonel John B. Campbell with 700 troops, including a detachment of Canadian Volunteers, landed at Dover (now Port Dover) on the north shore of Lake Erie. Claiming the town was inhabited by men who had taken part in the burning of Buffalo the previous year, Campbell burned Dover and several nearby settlements.

The following fall, Americans conducted a more ambitious raid into Upper Canada from Detroit. Departing on October 22, Brigadier General Duncan McArthur led 720 mounted regulars, volunteer militia, and Indians up the Thames River and then to the Grand River. McArthur's men lived off the land and burned mills and other buildings along the way. Heading south from the Grand, the raiders arrived near present-day Oakland, where on November 6 they defeated 400 inexperienced Canadian militia in the Battle of Malcolm's Mills. Casualties on both sides were slight in this engagement. Afterward, the raiders burned their way back to Detroit, where they arrived on November 17. It was the last military action of the war on the northern border.

The British were furious with this predatory warfare, although in truth it was little different from the kind of warfare they were waging in the Chesapeake. The major difference was that the British had a large fleet available to carry away their booty and thus preferred looting to burning.

107 | What happened on the Niagara frontier?

The United States launched its most ambitious campaign of the year on this front, and the result was some of the bloodiest and most memorable fighting of the war. Winfield Scott, now a brigadier general, prepared for the campaign in the spring by drilling his brigade seven hours a day for ten weeks at his camp near Buffalo. The American force swelled to around 5,500 in early summer with the arrival of other troops. Joining Scott on the Niagara front were additional regulars under the command of General Jacob Brown; volunteer militia from New York and Pennsylvania led by Brigadier General Peter B. Porter; a small band of Canadian Volunteers commanded by Joseph Willcocks; and some 500 Iroquois led by the aging Seneca leader Red Jacket.

Brown assumed command of the army and moved across the river on July 3 to lay siege to Fort Erie, which was defended by only 140 men under Major Thomas Buck. After offering token resistance, Buck surrendered the post. From Fort Erie, Brown ordered his force to head north along the Niagara River. Over the next two and a half months, there were four major battles: one each at Chippawa and Lundy's Lane and two at Fort Erie.

108 | What happened in the Battle of Chippawa?

As the Americans moved north along the Niagara River, they were met by the advance elements of a mixed British force of around 4,000 regulars, militia, and Indians under the command of Major General Phineas Riall (pronounced Rile). After some skirmishing on July 4, the two armies made camp, the British on the north side of the Chippawa River, the Americans on the south shore of nearby Street's Creek (now called Ussher's Creek).

The skirmishing resumed on July 5 when the British began moving men across the Chippawa. Militia and Indians led by Porter succeeded in driving back an Anglo-Indian force that threatened the American left flank, but a British counterattack forced these men to flee back to Street's Creek. Brown then dispatched Scott to meet a British force that was advancing from the north. In the ensuing Battle of Chippawa, which pitted 2,000 Americans against a British force of equal strength, the Americans prevailed because of well-placed artillery fire and the coolness that Scott's troops showed as they maneuvered under heavy British fire. After two hours, Riall realized that he was getting the worst of the exchange and ordered his men to withdraw to the north side of the Chippawa. The Americans had sustained 325 casualties, the British 500.

The Battle of Chippawa was an important benchmark in the war for the U.S. Army because it marked the first time that American regulars had defeated a British regular force of equal strength on an open battlefield. Scott's men were wearing gray jackets because the traditional blue cloth was unavailable, leading Riall to assume he was facing militia that he could easily brush aside. Stunned by the cool professionalism with which the American troops met his attack, a surprised Riall reportedly exclaimed, "Why, these are regulars!"[27] This remark entered U.S. Army lore for it seemed to prove that the once woeful American army had, through training and experience, become a fighting force worthy of the name.

109 | What happened in the Battle of Lundy's Lane?

Brown hoped to capitalize on the momentum of Chippawa and use logistical support from Chauncey's squadron to drive the British from the Niagara Peninsula. But Chauncey, preferring to concentrate on the rival British squadron on Lake Ontario, refused to cooperate. Brown was determined to attack anyway, but in the meantime General Gordon Drummond arrived at Fort George with British reinforcements and took command of all British troops there. Eager to engage the enemy, Drummond gradually moved his army to a hill at Lundy's Lane not far from Niagara Falls. Learning of the British presence, Brown ordered Scott to attack.

Scott arrived at Lundy's Lane on July 25 with about 1,200 men and confronted the British force, which then numbered about 1,600 men. Both sides sent in reinforcements so that in the end

This highly stylized print shows the climax of the Battle of Lundy's Lane, when Colonel James Miller (shown here on horseback) reached the British batteries on the crest of a hill. (Robert Tomes, Battles of America by Land and Sea.*)*

about 3,000 men were engaged on each side. The confused and bloody Battle of Lundy's Lane lasted six hours and dragged on into the night, drowning out the sound of Niagara Falls with the roar of artillery and rattle of musket fire.

Scott's men sustained heavy casualties from British artillery fire without getting close enough to use their muskets. To neutralize the British field guns, Colonel James Miller led a detachment close enough to fire a musket volley and then launched a bayonet charge. The British gunners were forced to retreat, and despite ferocious British counterattacks, the guns remained in American hands. Drummond also tried unsuccessfully to break the American line by launching several broader attacks. The battle ended when Brown ordered a withdrawal. By this time both sides were exhausted and unable to continue the fighting.

Colonel Miller characterized the Battle of Lundy's Lane as "one of the most desperately fought actions ever experienced in America," which was no exaggeration.[28] Each side suffered around 800 casualties, although the number of Americans killed (mainly from artillery fire) was twice that of the British. Scott's actions during the battle were little short of reckless, and his brigade sustained especially heavy casualties. In addition, all four senior officers—Drummond, Riall, Brown, and Scott—were wounded, and Riall was captured. The battle, the bloodiest of the war on the northern frontier, ended in a draw, although the British regained the field as well as their artillery when the Americans withdrew.

110 | What happened in the Battle of Fort Erie?

After Lundy's Lane, the Americans, now about 2,200 strong, withdrew to Fort Erie. Brigadier General Edmund P. Gaines, who took over for the wounded Brown, worked to enlarge the post so that it could accommodate this force. The fort was also greatly strengthened. Since a British attack was expected, Gaines kept his men on alert, and his vigilance paid off.

General Drummond first tried to force the evacuation of Fort Erie by attacking its supply bases at Black Rock and Buffalo. This effort failed when the force he sent across the river retreated after being ambushed on August 3 by American riflemen in the Battle of Conjocta Creek. The British were more successful nine days later when they surprised and captured two American schooners anchored off Fort Erie, the *Somers* (carrying 2 guns) and the *Ohio* (1 gun). That deprived the Americans at Fort Erie of artillery support from the river.

After trying to soften the fort with his artillery, Drummond launched a complicated and risky three-pronged attack with some 2,300 men after midnight on August 15. The plan went awry from the beginning when an Indian diversion on the west side of the fort began too late to attract any American interest. By then the main British assault, led by Lieutenant Colonel Victor Fischer, was already under way at the south end of the fort. That attack failed because Fischer's men were ordered to remove their flints to ensure surprise and were issued scaling ladders that were too short to get over the fort's walls. Deadly American small arms and artillery fire put an end to the assault, forcing Fischer to retreat.

Meanwhile, two smaller British forces led by Lieutenant Colonel William Drummond and Colonel Hercules Scott attacked the north end of the fort. The British managed to fight their way into one of the fort's bastions, and close combat ensued until the accidental detonation of a powder magazine in the fort blew the attacking force away. "The Explosion was tremendous," Gaines reported. "It was decisive."[29] The surviving British now withdrew, ending the battle. British losses in the three-pronged attack were 900, while the Americans lost only eighty-five.

111 | What was the sortie from Fort Erie?

In the month that followed the Battle of Fort Erie, the two sides exchanged artillery fire, and when General Gaines was wounded, General Brown, who was still recovering from his Lundy's Lane wounds, resumed command. When the British began erecting a battery within 500 yards of the fort, Brown's officers advised him to evacuate the post, but after 2,000 volunteer militia led by General Porter arrived, Brown decided that he would first make an attempt to knock out the British batteries.

On September 17, Porter and Colonel James Miller led a mixed force of around 2,000 regulars and militia against the British batteries. In the stormy weather they caught the British by surprise and spiked the guns in two batteries, but they soon ran into heavy resistance and were forced to withdraw. Casualties in the sortie from Fort Erie were heavy, about 500 for the United States and 700 for the British. As it happened, the British had already decided to withdraw to the north side of the Chippawa River, and thus soon after the sortie they decamped.

112 | What was the Battle of Cook's Mills?

Although the sortie from Fort Erie ended the major fighting on the Niagara frontier, there was one more engagement before the campaigning season ended. In early October, Major General George Izard arrived with a large force of well-trained regulars from Plattsburgh. Although he had no combat experience, Izard outranked Brown and took command of their combined force, some 6,000 men in all. Izard moved north from Fort Erie along the river road. Drummond was greatly outnumbered, but his position north of the Chippawa River was so strong that Izard dared not risk a frontal attack, and he could not draw Drummond into the open.

When Izard learned of a large stockpile of grain at Cook's Mills on Lyon's Creek (about twelve miles to the west), he sent Brigadier General Daniel Bissell and 900 men to capture or destroy it. Drummond responded by sending 750 men to intercept the Americans. On October 19, the opposing forces met in what is known as the Battle of Cook's Mills or the Battle of Lyon's Creek. Bissell used a frontal attack combined with a flanking movement to drive the British from the field. He then destroyed the grain he had come for. Casualties on both sides were fairly light, seventy-five for the United States and maybe thirty-five for the British. This was the last battle on the Niagara front in the war.

113 | What did the U.S. offensive on the Niagara frontier accomplish?

Not much. Despite the army lore, pride, and heroes that the campaign produced, the young republic had little to show for its efforts. Although it retained a toehold on the British side of the river, even this was given up before the year was out. On November 5, the United States blew up Fort Erie and returned to the American side of the river, leaving the British in full control of the west bank of the Niagara and still in command of Fort Niagara on the American side.

114 | Were there any significant naval battles on Lake Ontario in 1814?

No. The opposing commanders, Chauncey and Yeo, continued to be cautious, refusing to offer battle when at a disadvantage. Instead, both sides concentrated on building ever larger ships in the hope of achieving command of the lake. Dominance shifted back and forth until September, when the British launched the ship-of-the-line *St. Lawrence* (104 guns) from their shipyard in Kingston. She set sail on her maiden voyage on October 16 and gave the British naval superiority on Lake Ontario for the rest of the war.

Despite its shallow draft and flimsy construction, the *St. Lawrence* had more firepower than any other ship in the Royal Navy. The British had two other ships-of-the-line under construction at Kingston, the *Canada* and the *Wolfe,* and the United States had two at Sackets Harbor, the *Chippewa* and the *New Orleans.* Had the war lasted another year, the world might have seen five of the world's most powerful ships in service on Lake Ontario.

115 | What happened in the Battle of Oswego?

Although no major naval battles were fought on Lake Ontario, the British squadron there targeted several American sites on the shore, most notably Oswego. The town, protected by Fort Ontario, was a vital link in the supply line to Sackets Harbor. War materiel, naval stores, and provisions were shipped from New York City up the Hudson River to the Mohawk River and forwarded west on the Mohawk to a series of connecting waterways that terminated in Oswego on Lake Ontario. From Oswego supplies were ferried along the lakeshore to Sackets Harbor.

In early May the British took advantage of temporary naval superiority on Lake Ontario to launch an attack on Oswego. Commodore Yeo's squadron ferried some 900 men, mostly soldiers and marines under the command of General Drummond, from Kingston to Oswego, which was defended by 500 regulars and militia commanded by Lieutenant Colonel George E. Mitchell. Contrary winds and American artillery fire drove them off on May 5, but the following day they returned and defeated the troops that met them on the shore and those remaining in Fort Ontario. The British sustained ninety casualties in the exchange, the Americans about half this number, although some twenty-five Americans were captured. The raid netted some naval guns, ammunition, naval stores, and food, but the British missed a much larger cache of naval guns and rope that was in storage twelve miles up the Oswego River at Oswego Falls (now Fulton, New York).

116 | What happened in the Battle of Sandy Creek?

The guns and rope that survived the British raid upon Oswego were desperately needed at Sackets Harbor to outfit ships, and

Master Commandant Melancthon Woolsey sought to ferry them to Sackets in a number of boats. Hoping to evade detection by the British squadron nearby, Woolsey left Oswego on May 29 at night and guided his flotilla north along the shore. Early the next morning, he took refuge in Sandy Creek. Here the flotilla was protected by 130 U.S. Riflemen under Major Daniel Appling, 300 troops who arrived from Sackets Harbor with some field artillery, and 120 Oneida Indians.

Later that day Captain Stephen Popham led a force of 200 soldiers, marines, and seamen from the British squadron up Sandy Creek in search of the American flotilla. Spotting the masts of the American boats, Popham landed some men on shore and advanced upriver with artillery from his boats offering covering fire. The Oneida fled from the British artillery, but the U.S. Riflemen, with support from American artillery, cut down the advancing British and forced Popham to surrender. The British had sustained seventy casualties, the Americans and the Indians only two. American success in the Battle of Sandy Creek not only preserved the naval guns and rope for the United States, but the loss of the boats induced Commodore Yeo to call off his planned attack on Sackets Harbor.

117 | What was the great Rope Walk of 1814?

With Yeo's squadron still hovering nearby, the Americans moved their cargo from Sandy Creek overland by wagon to Sackets Harbor twenty miles away. But a huge rope or cable—300 feet long, seven inches in diameter, and weighing 9,600 pounds—was too large and heavy for any wagon. Since the rope was needed to outfit a heavy frigate under construction, it was essential to get it to Sackets Harbor. At this point, Colonel Allen Clark's 55th Regiment of New York militia volunteered to carry the cable. On

June 9 part of the rope was put into the largest wagon available, while the rest was lifted by the men, perhaps a hundred in all, and carried on their shoulders. The men marched for a mile at a time and then rested. Their shoulders became so raw that they had to pad them with straw and grass. When some men dropped out along the way, others took their place. The march took thirty hours. When the rope arrived at Sackets with the cable, the men were feted with a barrel of whiskey and awarded $2 a day in bonus pay.

118 | Why did the British invade New York?

Because it lay south of Montreal, they could bring considerable force to bear and mount a powerful offensive. In fact, the British sent an army ten thousand strong into the United States, the largest ever to invade American territory. Sir George Prevost, the governor general of Canada, took direct command of this invasion. His orders from the British government were to seize and hold as much of upper New York as was feasible but to make sure that he was not cut off the way that General John Burgoyne had been in 1777 during the American Revolution. Buttressed with reinforcements that included veteran units and several of Wellington's best generals from the Peninsular War, Prevost amassed his army at Montreal at the end of August. The Americans could not offer much resistance to a force of this size because Secretary of War John Armstrong had ordered General Izard and some 4,000 men to march to the Niagara frontier. That left Brigadier General Alexander Macomb as the ranking officer at Plattsburgh, and he could muster only 3,400 men.

Prevost advanced into New York, sweeping aside militia and bypassing trees that had been felled to impede his progress. After reaching the north side of the Saranac River at Plattsburgh with about 8,000 men, Prevost engaged the enemy across the river and sent a detachment west to outflank Macomb's army on the south side of the river. Although the Battle of Plattsburgh was now under way, Prevost waited to launch an all-out attack until his flanking movement had been completed and he knew the outcome of a nearby naval battle on Lake Champlain.

119 | What happened in the Battle of Lake Champlain?

The British had established control over Lake Champlain the previous year when they captured two American warships, the *Eagle* and the *Growler*, each mounting eleven guns. Since then both sides had been furiously building warships, and by the time Prevost reached Plattsburgh the two squadrons were about evenly matched. The British squadron, headed by Captain George Downie, included the *Confiance* (which mounted 39 guns and served as Downie's flagship), three smaller warships, and twelve gunboats. The American squadron, commanded by Master Commandant Thomas Macdonough, included his flagship *Saratoga* (carrying 26 guns), three smaller warships, and ten gunboats. Downie's squadron had the advantage in long guns, but Macdonough's carronades gave him the advantage at close range.

Macdonough anchored his squadron south of Cumberland Head near Plattsburgh. The prevailing winds favored him because they made it difficult for Downie to stand off and make the best use of his long guns. In addition, Macdonough put out the *Saratoga*'s kedge anchors, which made it possible for him to maneuver the ship without using his sails. As it happened, this gave him a decisive advantage in the battle that ensued.

On September 11, Downie rounded Cumberland Head and sailed for the American squadron. Macdonough used his long guns to good effect as the British squadron approached, but Downie closed in good order, and soon the opposing squadrons were fully engaged. The heaviest fighting was between the two flagships, which exchanged broadside after broadside. Downie was killed fifteen minutes into the battle, his flattened watch marking the exact time of his death. Macdonough was knocked down by the flying head of a decapitated midshipman. Although momentarily dazed, he sustained no serious injury.

When almost all of the *Saratoga*'s guns facing the enemy were knocked out of action, Macdonough performed the masterstroke of the battle, using his kedge anchors to wind his ship around and bring fresh batteries into action. Lieutenant James Robertson, who had succeeded Downie, tried to wind the *Confiance* around, but without advance preparation his lines became fouled, and the *Saratoga* pummeled the now immobile British ship into submission. According to Robertson, "The Ship's Company declared they would stand no longer to their Quarters, nor could the Officers with their utmost exertions rally them."[30] Two and a half hours into the battle, the *Confiance* surrendered, and the rest of the British warships followed suit. Only the gunboats (which had fled earlier) escaped. This marked the end of the Battle of Lake Champlain. Macdonough's victory over the British squadron was every bit as complete as Perry's on Lake Erie the year before.

120 | What was the impact of the U.S. victory on Lake Champlain?

It had a decisive effect on the land battle then under way at Plattsburgh. When Prevost learned of Downie's defeat, he feared that American control of Lake Champlain could threaten his supply lines and enable the United States to land troops behind him and cut off any retreat. He therefore ordered a general withdrawal.

The order reached the troops flanking Macdonough's force just as they were about to attack the Americans from the rear.

There was considerable grumbling in the British ranks over the decision to withdraw. Prevost had already alienated many of the officers who had served in the Peninsular War because (unlike Wellington) he insisted on a strict dress code. These officers now combined in open criticism of the governor with Commodore Yeo and other naval officers, who insisted that Prevost had forced Downie into action before his squadron was ready. Many civilians in Canada who disliked Prevost also joined in the hue and cry. "All ranks of people," reported a British newspaper, "were clamorous against Sir George Prevost."[31] Prevost was recalled to Great Britain but died before he could make a case for himself.

The invasion of New York was the last major military operation on the northern frontier. With the end of this campaign, both sides went into winter quarters. The American victory on the lake, which had produced the British retreat on land, was significant because it left the British without a major victory in this important theater and thus without a significant slice of American territory that might be used as a bargaining chip in the peace negotiations then under way.

121 | How did the British use their naval power in 1814?

In a host of different ways. They extended their naval blockade to New England in April, and they increased their raids up and down the coast. They occupied part of Maine (which was then a district in Massachusetts) and stepped up their depredations in the Chesapeake. In addition, they mounted major operations against Washington, Baltimore, and Alexandria.

122 | Why did the British extend their blockade to New England?

Because they were now in the driver's seat in the war, they no longer needed to favor anti-war New England. Nor did they need the grain that New England merchants had earlier shipped to British armies in the Spanish Peninsula. They also wanted to prevent American warships and privateers from using New England's ports. Finally, they were determined to bring the war home to Americans all along the Atlantic seaboard, and not simply those living in the middle and southern states.

123 | Did the expanded British blockade hurt the United States?

Yes, but it could have been worse had the economy-minded Admiralty been willing to devote more ships to blockade duty. Still, the effect, especially on the economy and government revenue, was bad enough. American trade (exports plus imports), which had declined from $115 million in 1811 to $50 million in 1813, fell to $20 million in 1814, the lowest level for any year since the government had begun keeping records in 1790. The gluts and shortages that had appeared the previous year only got worse in 1814 because foreign and coastal trade continued to shrink. Many people whose livelihood was tied to the sea faced ruin.

The blockade also had a profound impact on the nation's finances. Congress had doubled the customs duties (taxes on imports) at the start of the war, but government income had remained flat at $14 million from 1811 to 1813 and then had plummeted to $11 million in 1814. With the cost of the war soaring while government revenue was shrinking, the administration found itself in dire financial straits.

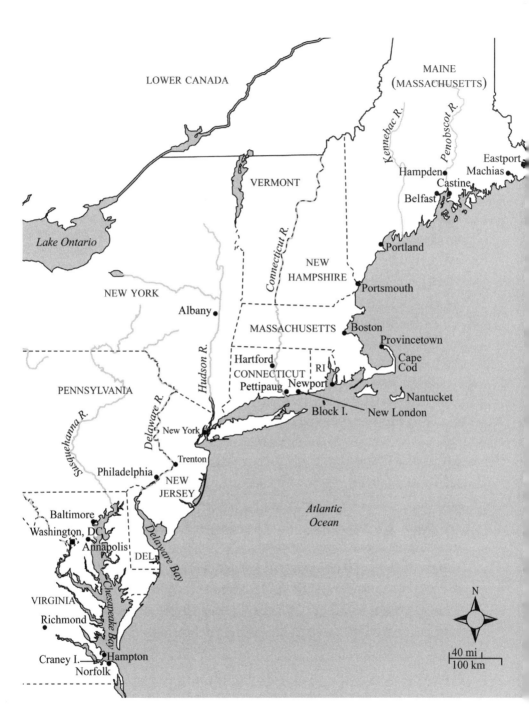

The War on the Atlantic Coast.

124 | What happened to Nantucket and Block Island?

They had little choice but to come to terms with the British because trade and fishing were their life's blood. Nantucket, off the coast of Massachusetts, was reliably Republican, but to survive its people had to be able to fish in nearby waters and import necessities from the mainland. In August 1814, the island declared its neutrality, agreeing to surrender its public stores to the British and to supply the Royal Navy in exchange for being permitted to fish and trade. Block Island, off the coast of Rhode Island, did not go quite so far, but it was supplying the Royal Navy with so much food and intelligence that the U.S. government prohibited all trade with the island.

125 | What was the purpose of the British raids on the Atlantic Coast?

The British still hoped that these raids would force the United States to redeploy regulars from the northern frontier, although that never happened. They also wanted to bring the war home to Americans and retaliate for American depredations in Upper Canada. Beyond this, they expected to earn substantial prize money by raiding the largely undefended and yet prosperous coastal settlements.

After the burning of Dover and nearby settlements, Sir George Prevost asked Vice Admiral Sir Alexander Cochrane, who had succeeded Sir John Borlase Warren on the American station, to "assist in inflicting that measure of retaliation which shall deter the enemy from a repetition of similar outrages."[32] Cochrane had little love for Americans and thus no reservations about complying with Prevost's request, but he realized that the Royal Navy was dependent on Americans for food and other necessities. Privately he authorized his officers to spare those settlements that paid tribute or supplied British warships.

Many of the British raids were small-scale affairs that singled out a farm or plantation or a small settlement, but some involved sizeable squadrons in significant operations. In April a British squadron ventured up the Connecticut River to Pettipaug (now Essex, Connecticut) and destroyed twenty-seven vessels valued at $140,000. In August the Royal Navy pounded Stonington, Connecticut. New England, heretofore exempt from depredations, now felt the full force of the Royal Navy's power.

126 | Why did the British occupy Maine?

Because it was an easy target and acquiring territory there might enable Britain to rectify the international boundary and establish a direct land route between Quebec and Halifax. Maine, which was then part of Massachusetts, was wedged between Lower Canada and New Brunswick, and the Treaty of Paris at the end of the American Revolution had left that portion of the Canadian-American boundary in dispute.

On July 11 a British force of 1,000 men under Lieutenant Colonel Andrew Pilkington sailed into Passamaquoddy Bay and seized control of Moose Island, which was claimed by both nations but occupied by the United States. Fort Sullivan, garrisoned by eighty-five men under Major Perley Putnam, offered little resistance before surrendering.

The British followed up six weeks later with a much larger amphibious operation aimed at Penobscot Bay. On September 1, Rear Admiral Edward Griffith ferried 2,500 men under the command of Sir John Sherbrooke, the lieutenant governor of Nova Scotia, into the bay. Sherbrooke seized Castine and then sent a force up the Penobscot River, forcing Captain Charles Morris of the U.S. Navy to burn the *Adams,* a 28-gun sloop, before fleeing with his men. Later the British occupied Machias, which gave them effective control over a hundred miles of the Maine coast. The British seized all public property in the occupied territory and some private property as well. This part of Maine remained in British hands until the war ended.

127 | How did Americans respond to the occupation of Maine?

Even though Maine was Republican, many of the residents, perhaps even a majority, did not object to the British presence because the local economy boomed. The illicit trade with Canada that Mainers had conducted in defiance of American customs officials was now carried on openly, mostly by sea. In addition, Castine became a resort town for British army and naval officers on leave, and the hard cash they spent lubricated the local economy.

Claiming that Moose Island belonged to Great Britain, Royal officials insisted that all residents there take an oath of allegiance to the Crown or leave. Most took the oath. Elsewhere residents had a different choice: take an oath to keep the peace or leave. Few had any objection to this innocuous oath and willingly took it. The British also offered American residents an additional option. If they took the same oath of allegiance required on Moose Island, they would secure all the commercial privileges that were accorded to British subjects. This meant they could trade freely with British ports in Canada and elsewhere without fear of molestation from the Royal Navy. The lure of this trade was too attractive for some Americans to resist.

U.S. officials halted all trade and mail service to the occupied territory and hatched a plan of re-conquest that called for sending a mixed force of regulars and militia overland to attack Castine from the rear. Even under the best of circumstances, this dubious plan was unlikely to succeed. It would not be easy to support a large force moving through the interior, nor would it be easy to keep the operation secret. The plan also required the cooperation of Caleb Strong, the Federalist governor of Massachusetts, who was expected to supply the militia and provide part of the funding. Strong demurred because the state was strapped for cash, and also because his advisors warned that the operation was unlikely to succeed without naval control of Penobscot Bay. The plan had to be shelved anyway when it was leaked to the press.

128 | Were there any fresh ideas for counting British depredations on the coast?

Yes, a few. In the Chesapeake, Captain Joshua Barney, a former naval officer and successful privateer commander, persuaded the Navy Department to give him authority to establish a flotilla of barges and gunboats that could harass British warships and fight their smaller boats in shallow waters. Barney's Chesapeake flotilla went into action in the spring of 1814 and over the next three months enjoyed considerable success, forcing the Royal Navy to devote significant resources to counter the threat. Barney finally had to burn his boats above Pig Point on the Patuxent on August 22, 1814, to prevent them from falling into British hands.

129 | Why was Washington, D.C., so vulnerable in 1814?

American leaders did not think the British would target the nation's capital and were slow to prepare any plan of defense. Secretary of War John Armstrong, who thought Baltimore a far more likely target, was especially remiss. On July 1, President Madison created a new military district embracing the capital headed by General William Winder. Overwhelmed by the task before him, Winder seemed unable to focus on the defense of Washington, and the city remained vulnerable.

130 | What happened at the Battle of Bladensburg?

On August 19–20, Major General Robert Ross landed a British force of about 4,000 men at Benedict, Maryland, and followed the Patuxent River inland. He was joined by Rear Admiral Cockburn, who had overseen the predatory raids in the Chesapeake the previous summer and who now persuaded Ross to continue on to Washington. To halt their advance, the United States assembled 6,000 men at Bladensburg, but except for 600 seamen and Marines under Captain Barney, who had sped to Washington after the destruction of his flotilla, and 500 regulars under Lieutenant Colonel William Scott, most of the men were raw militia. According to one British officer, the Americans "seemed [like] country people, who would have been much more appropriately employed in attending to their agricultural occupations than in standing, with their muskets, in their hands."[33] To make matters worse, Secretary of State James Monroe, who had no military authority, weakened the American lines by redeploying the troops.

The British army arrived just as the last Americans fell into line on August 24. Despite heavy casualties, the British got across the bridge and swept the militia before them. Winder, who radiated defeatism from the outset, ordered the militia to pull back, but this turned into a rout that was dubbed "the Bladensburg races." Only Barney's men, who were manning large guns they had hauled into the field, held firm, taking a heavy toll on the British with grapeshot before being overwhelmed. Barney was wounded in the action and taken captive, and by 4:00 that afternoon Ross was in command of the field. The British had suffered far more casualties, 250 to seventy, but they had nonetheless prevailed.

131 | How did the U.S. defeat at Bladensburg affect Washington, D.C.?

Panic gripped the city. Already people were fleeing the capital, and that exodus accelerated when news of the defeat arrived. The British rested for several hours after the battle, which gave those who had not yet left more time to do so. Dolley Madison took it upon herself to oversee the removal of White House treasures, including a large portrait of George Washington by Gilbert Stuart, even though doing so meant sacrificing her personal property. Other federal officials took what property they could, and the city remained without a federal presence for two days.

132 | What did the British do when they reached Washington?

By the time the British marched into Washington around 8:00 p.m. on August 24, it was almost a ghost town. There was considerable looting, not by British soldiers, who, as usual were kept on a tight leash, but by locals who remained behind to take advantage of the situation. The British looked for someone to surrender the city, but no one in authority could be found.

Ross and Cockburn led a group of British officers into the White House. After consuming some food and wine that had been laid out for the president's usual afternoon meal and taking a few souvenirs, the British set fire to the building. They also burned the Capitol, including the Library of Congress, and several other public buildings. Dr. William Thornton, the superintendent of patents, persuaded the British to spare the patent office because it was filled with privately-owned "models of the arts ... useful to all mankind."[34] With a few exceptions, the British left most homes and other private property alone. Captain Thomas Tingey burned the Washington Naval Yard and two ships that were on the stocks to keep them out of British hands.

The fires in Washington burned all night and could be seen from miles away. The next day the city was stricken by a pair of storms. That same day, August 25, the British decamped, marching back to Benedict, where they re-boarded their waiting ships.

133 | Why did the British burn Washington?

Under the rules of war, they were entitled to seize or destroy any public property, although they were criticized on both sides of the Atlantic for burning government buildings that were not being used for military purposes. Conventional wisdom holds that the British were retaliating for the destruction of the public buildings in York the year before, but it seems more likely that they were complying with Prevost's request to retaliate for the destruction of Dover and other towns in Upper Canada.

134 | What happened at Alexandria?

Although Alexandria was Federalist and more than 100 miles up the Potomac River, it was not beyond the long reach of the Royal Navy. As part of the Washington campaign, Captain James Gordon sailed a squadron up the Potomac, fighting contrary winds and shallow waters that grounded some of his ships. When he threatened Fort Washington, the post commander, Captain Samuel T. Dyson, blew up the fort and fled. For this he was later cashiered from the army. When Gordon reached Alexandria on

The successful defense of Fort McHenry spared Baltimore from naval assault and produced "The Star-Spangled Banner." Depicted here is the British bombardment on Fort McHenry. (Painting by Alfred J. Miller. Maryland Historical Society.)

August 29, the affluent city, eager to escape destruction, formally surrendered, delivering up all its public stores and maritime property. Gordon had to fight his way downriver, unloading and then reloading some ships that ran aground, but he made it back to the British fleet with twenty-one prizes loaded with booty. One British naval officer called Gordon's feat "as brilliant an achievement . . . as grace the annals of our naval history."[35] As for Alexandria, she was sharply criticized for not putting up a fight.

135 | Why did the British target Baltimore?

Baltimore was the most ardently pro-Republican, pro-war, and anti-British city in the nation. It was also the home port for many of the privateers that had been preying on British commerce. The British knew about its reputation and were eager to punish the city. "I do not like to contemplate scenes of blood and destruction," said one British naval officer, "but my heart is deeply interested in the coercion of these Baltimore heroes, who are perhaps the most inveterate against us of all the Yankees."[36] Another reason was that it was the third largest city in the United States and an important commercial hub. Its warehouses were loaded with goods and commodities that would yield considerable prize money.

136 | What was the Battle of North Point?

It took almost three weeks after the destruction of Washington for General Ross to get his army into action against Baltimore. On September 12, about 4,500 British soldiers and seamen landed at North Point and began the march to Baltimore fourteen miles away. Blocking the road en route was a force of 3,200 militia commanded by Brigadier General John Stricker. In the ensuing engagement, known as the Battle of North Point, Ross was killed when he rode ahead to scout the enemy. The loss of this popular and talented officer put a pall over the entire British operation. Ross was succeeded in command by Colonel Arthur Brooke, who softened up Stricker's militia with artillery and then ordered a frontal attack that drove the Americans from the field. The battle was a bloody one: The British lost 340 men, the Americans 215.

After resting for the night, the British resumed their march toward Baltimore. When they reached the outskirts, Brooke realized how difficult breaching the well-manned American defenses would be. Ever since 1813, Major General Samuel Smith, a U.S. senator and head of the city's militia, had been working to strengthen Baltimore's defenses. After the fall of Washington, he put every available person, black as well as white, free as well as slave, to the task of building earthworks. To man the works, Smith amassed a formidable force, some 15,000 men, most of whom were citizen soldiers.

137 | Why did the Royal Navy bombard Fort McHenry?

To support the British army's assault on Baltimore. Before they could get close enough to use their guns on the American lines, British warships first had to silence the guns of Fort McHenry, a star-shaped coastal fortification that commanded the entrance to Baltimore's harbor. The fort was manned by 1,000 men commanded by Major George Armistead. On September 13, Admiral Cochrane personally led a British squadron of bomb and rocket ships up the Patapsco River. Over the next twenty-five hours, Cochrane's ships pounded the fort with 1,500 rounds of solid shot, explosive shells, and Congreve rockets. Only 400 of these rounds found their mark, and the defenders inside the fort sustained only four killed and twenty-four wounded. When a nighttime flanking operation also failed, Cochrane notified the army that he could not provide naval support for an assault on Baltimore. By this time, Brooke realized that he could expect no help from the Royal Navy and was marching his men back to the British ships. The failure of the assault on Fort McHenry meant that Baltimore was spared.

138 | Why was "The Star-Spangled Banner" written?

Francis Scott Key, a lawyer from Georgetown in the District of Columbia, had taken a truce ship to the British fleet to secure the release of a civilian prisoner of war before the attack on Fort McHenry. Although he accomplished his mission, British naval officials would not let him leave lest he warn of the impending attack. He spent the night pacing the deck of his truce ship under the guns of the main British fleet while watching the bombardment of the fort by the detached squadron nine miles away. The next morning, when he realized that the attacking squadron was withdrawing and saw (probably with a spyglass) the large American flag (thirty by forty-two feet) run up, he realized the defenders had prevailed. Key was so moved that he wrote a song set to a British drinking tune, "To Anacreon in Heaven," that was popular on both sides of the Atlantic. "The Rockets' red glare" mentioned in the Key's song were Congreve rockets. "The Bombs bursting in air" were explosive shells designed to go off just before hitting the ground.

Initially entitled "The Defence of Fort McHenry," the song was first published in a handbill and then in newspapers up and down the coast. Renamed "The Star-Spangled Banner," it proved to be an instant hit that gradually nudged aside other patriotic airs, such as "Hail Columbia" and "Yankee Doodle." In 1931 Congress designated it as the national anthem.

139 | What became of the Fort McHenry flag?

The flag remained in the Armistead family for the rest of the century. It was occasionally displayed, and in 1907 it was lent to the Smithsonian, a loan that was converted into a gift five years later. By this time the flag was missing a star and was eight feet shorter on the fly end because so many swatches had been cut off and given away as souvenirs. The flag is now on display in a special climate-controlled glass case. It is one of the Smithsonian's most treasured artifacts and the nation's best-known relic from the War of 1812.

140 | What was the Battle of Caulk's Field?

It was a little-known battle fought on Maryland's Eastern Shore on August 31 as part of the campaign to capture Baltimore.

To deter militia on the Eastern Shore from coming to the aid of Baltimore, Admiral Cochrane ordered Sir Peter Parker, a promising young naval officer and scion of a distinguished naval family, to carry out a diversion. Sailing to the Eastern Shore, Parker learned from a runaway slave that there was a militia camp two and a half miles from modern day Fairlee, Maryland. With some 250 seamen and marines, he decided to attack it.

Learning of the British approach, Lieutenant Colonel Philip Reed, a Revolutionary War veteran and former U.S. senator, quickly deployed the 200 militia in his camp. Reed himself headed a group of riflemen who harassed the British from a grove of trees as they approached and then fell back to the main American line, which was anchored by several field pieces. The British took heavy fire and broke off the engagement just as the Americans ran out of ammunition and were about to retreat. The British sustained forty casualties to only three for the Americans. Among the British victims was Parker, who bled to death from a deep thigh wound.

The Battle of Caulk's Field had no effect on the battle for Baltimore across the bay, but it was a rare case when American militia had defeated a larger British force (although it was a naval force rather than British regulars). When word of the victory spread, it gave a small boost to American morale. The battle also deprived the Royal Navy of one of its rising stars, who was eulogized in a poem by his cousin, Lord Byron.

141 | Did the American war on British commerce continue in 1814?

Yes, it did. There were no naval engagements on the high seas of much significance in 1814, but three U.S. sloops that had been built for speed—the *Hornet* (mounting 20 guns), the *Peacock* (22 guns), and the *Wasp* (22 guns)—managed to get to sea, where they preyed on British commerce. So, too, did a number of American privateers. "The depredations committed on our commerce by American ships of war and privateers," complained the *Naval Chronicle,* "[have] attained an extent beyond all former precedent."[37]

The waters around the British Isles offered especially lucrative opportunities for privateers. "In the chops of the Channel . . . in our own seas," said a member of Parliament, "American privateers had come and carried off our vessels."[38] Although the war in Europe was now over, French officials nonetheless allowed American cruisers to bring their prizes into their ports. The Admiralty did not have enough small and fast warships to chase down American privateers, and with insurance rates in British waters rising, merchants bombarded the government with complaints.

The *Prince-de-Neufchatel* (17 guns) enjoyed a particularly successful cruise, taking or destroying $1 million dollars in British property. The *Governor Tompkins* (14 guns) and *Harpy* (14 guns) also did well. The former plundered and burned fourteen prizes in the English Channel, while the latter captured prizes valued at $400,000. Captain Thomas Boyle, commander of the privateer *Chasseur* (16 guns)—known as "the Pride of Baltimore"—mocked British naval blockades by sending the captain of a ship he had just captured into a British port on August 27 to deliver a proclamation that announced a blockade of "all the ports, harbours, bays, creeks, rivers, inlets, outlets, islands, and sea coast of the United Kingdom of G. Britain and Ireland."[39]

Even when cornered by British warships, some privateers successfully defended themselves. On September 27, the *General Armstrong* (9 guns) inflicted 200 casualties when attacked by boats from British warships in the Azores. The privateer had to be abandoned, but it lost only nine men in the engagement. Similarly, on October 11, when the *Prince-de-Neufchatel* (17 guns) was becalmed off Nantucket and attacked by boats from the British frigate *Endymion* (47 guns), it inflicted at least sixty-five casualties on the British while losing only thirty of its crew. The American privateer then made it safely back to an American port with prize goods valued at $200,000.

142 | What was the public reaction to the outcome of the campaign of 1814?

On both sides of the Atlantic, it was mixed, although the British had more reason to celebrate. Americans could take pride in the performance of their regulars on the Niagara front, the defeat of a British squadron on Lake Champlain and the preservation of upper New York, the defense of Baltimore, and the continued success of their privateers at sea. The British, on the other hand, had tightened their blockade and stepped up their raids on the American coast. They had also beaten back the American offensive on the Niagara, occupied Maine, and burned the young republic's capital. With the British amassing forces in North America faster than the United States could, the momentum of the war continued to shift in their favor.

CHAPTER FIVE

The End of the War

143 | What was the crisis of 1814?

By the end of 1814, the United States faced a host of problems that threatened its ability to prosecute the war. The army and the navy were plagued by difficulties; the nation's ability to finance the war was deteriorating; there was growing trade with the enemy; and Federalist opposition to the war in New England was becoming ever more strident. Together, these problems suggested that the young and fragile republic was in the throes of a crisis, one that threatened not simply its ability to wage war against such a powerful foe, but also its very future as a nation.

144 | What problems did the U.S. Army face?

There was no doubt that the army was getting better with experience, but recruitment continued to lag behind its needs. To boost recruiting, Congress increased army pay and began offering a premium to anyone who secured a recruit. In addition, it had boosted the enlistment bounty from $12 in December 1811 to $124 and 160 acres of land in January 1814. Even so, the army, which had an authorized level of 62,500 in early 1814, had only around 45,000 men in service at the end of the year, which meant that the ranks were only about three-quarters full.

The army was beset by other woes. The supply system remained chaotic and undependable, and the lack of sufficient revenue only made the problem worse. Troops were often without adequate clothing or lodging and went hungry and unpaid. Although by law army pay was supposed to be no more than two months in arrears, by the fall of 1814 many troops had not been paid in six or even twelve months.

The conditions of service contributed to another problem, widespread desertion. Almost 13 percent of the enlisted men deserted during the war, and half of the desertions occurred in 1814. Many men left because they were hungry, unpaid, ill, or homesick, but, because of generous bounties, the army also had to contend with a growing number of bounty jumpers—men who enlisted, accepted the first portion of the bounty (which was $50), and then disappeared, only to enlist again elsewhere.

President Madison issued proclamations in 1812 and again in 1814 pardoning any deserters who returned to their units within three months, but this did not have much effect. The War Department offered a $50 bounty for the capture of deserters, but punishing those who were caught posed a problem. The army wanted to deter desertion, but being overly harsh would discourage enlistments. In practice, the army was often (although not always) lenient with first-time offenders and reserved execution for repeat offenders, especially bounty-jumpers. Nonetheless, executions steadily rose during the war, from three in 1812, to thirty-two in 1813, to 146 in 1814.

Not only did the army have to contend with desertion in the ranks, it also experienced dissension in the officer corps. Feuding officers sometimes refused to support one another in the field. The feud between generals James Wilkinson and Wade Hampton in the ill-starred campaign against Montreal in 1813 was only the most notorious of many such disputes that undermined field operations. In addition, some officers sought to settle their differences with a duel. By 1814, such "interviews of honor" had become so common that the War Department had to threaten duelists with dismissal from the service.

145 | What problems did the U.S. Navy face?

The navy had been a crack service from the beginning of the war, with excellent officers, well-trained men, good equipment, and fine ships. But it had always had to compete with privateers for men, and by 1814 it faced additional recruiting obstacles. Potential recruits knew that most of the larger ships would be unable to get to sea, and few wanted to serve on the lakes or in the gunboats or barges assigned to coastal defense. Plus, the army siphoned off some experienced sailors with its generous bounties. Fully 5 percent of all men who served in the U.S. Army during the war were seamen.

146 | What was the state of American public finances?

Bad and getting worse. Secretary of the Treasury Albert Gallatin had devised a plan in early 1812 that called for financing normal government operations and interest on the war loans out of current income while borrowing to cover the cost of the war. But with revenue from the duties on trade likely to decline while the cost of servicing the national debt climbed, new taxes were essential. Congress had doubled the import duties shortly after the declaration of war but had put off adopting the internal (excise) taxes that Gallatin had said were necessary. These taxes were not finally adopted until a year into the war and did not go into effect until six months later. As a result, the government's financial position steadily worsened, making it harder to borrow money and forcing it to resort to a form of paper money known as treasury notes, which were one-year interest-bearing notes.

In the summer of 1814, the entire system of war finance collapsed. The government was unable to borrow the money it needed, and most banks and contractors would no longer accept treasury notes. U.S. bonds dropped to 75 percent of their nominal value and were quoted as low as 60 percent in Boston. Treasury notes also lost 15 to 25 percent of their value and sometimes could not be disposed of at any price.

The collapse of public finance led to a host of problems. Military recruiting came to a standstill in some areas because there were no funds, and some new recruits refused to march until they had received the first portion of their bounty. The armory in Springfield, Massachusetts, was idled for lack of funds, and there was not enough money to take care of prisoners of war in New England or to purchase medical supplies needed on the northern frontier. In some cases, government officials and contractors borrowed money on their own signatures to get badly needed supplies.

The government was also unable to service the national debt. Although by law interest on the national debt had to be paid quarterly in specie (gold or silver), the Treasury had to offer treasury notes to bondholders in the fall of 1814. In effect, the United States defaulted on the national debt. Ironically, bondholders overseas got paid because the nation's international banker, Baring Brothers & Company in London, advanced the necessary funds. By the end of the war, the Treasury owed Baring $200,000.

147 | What was the state of U.S. banks?

Compounding the nation's financial woes was the collapse of the nation's banking system in the summer of 1814. Banks in those days issued their own notes, which served as a local currency. Although the National Bank had once kept the state-chartered banks in check, Congress had refused to re-charter the National Bank in 1811, forcing it to close down. The number of state banks proliferated, and the value of notes they put into circulation soared. At the same time, the amount of specie in the United States was declining. When the National Bank closed its doors, $7 million in specie was sent overseas to foreign holders of bank stock. Specie also flowed from the middle and southern states into New England and from there into Canada to pay for British goods that were smuggled into the country. With their note issues expanding and their specie reserves shrinking, many state-chartered banks found themselves in a precarious position.

The British invasion of the Chesapeake in the summer of 1814 created a run on the banks in Washington and Baltimore, forcing them to suspend specie payments. Other banks in the middle and southern states followed suit, and eventually those in the West did, too. Only the banks in New England, which had greater specie reserves and tighter banking laws, remained solvent, but they had to drastically cut back on their loans. With the suspension of specie payments, bank paper lost much of its nominal value, and banks would no longer honor one another's notes.

The suspension of specie payments created a credit crunch that slowed economic activity. It also created problems for the federal government. With banks refusing to honor one another's notes, it was difficult for the Treasury to transfer funds from one part of the country to another. Government funds accumulated in some areas while being depleted in others. Moreover, because the Treasury accepted depreciated bank notes at par in the payment of taxes and the fulfillment of loan contracts, the federal government received less than full value.

148 | How widespread was American trade with the enemy?

Very widespread. Congress had enacted an enemy trade act in 1812, but it proved ineffective. The British needed large quantities of food to feed their military and naval forces serving in North

America, and Americans had a voracious appetite for British goods. Hence, there was a steady flow of goods in both directions, especially across the long and largely undefended Canadian frontier. "From the St. Lawrence to the [Atlantic] Ocean," declared General George Izard in July 1814, "an open Disregard prevails for the Laws prohibiting Intercourse with the Enemy."[40]

Because the war had disrupted so many other economic activities and British purchasing agents paid in cash, Americans—Federalists and Republicans alike—were willing to supply the enemy's needs. Americans routinely supplied British warships on the Atlantic coast, and the quantity of American foodstuffs that flowed into Canada steadily grew during the war. "Two-thirds of the army in Canada," boasted Sir George Prevost in August 1814, "are at this moment eating beef provided by American contractors."[41]

Some of this trade was carried on by small vessels sailing along the coast into occupied Maine or Canada, but most of the goods moved by land or water across the northern border. Even with assistance from the army and navy, it was nearly impossible for U.S. customs collectors to stamp out this trade. The smugglers simply had too many advantages. The territory was vast, the wilderness dense, and almost everywhere local residents had an interest in the trade and thus sided with the smugglers. Customs officials seeking to enforce the law often met with violence, occasionally even death, and invariably they received a chilly reception when they sought justice in the local courts.

149 | What did the federal government do to address the crisis of 1814?

The government adopted a variety of measures in the winter of 1814–15 to address the crisis at hand. To boost army enlistments, the bounty was increased from $124 and 160 acres of land to $124 and 320 acres. Since unskilled laborers normally earned only $10–20 a month, the new bounty was probably the equivalent of two years of wages, perhaps $30,000 today. Congress considered (but rejected) conscripting militia for two years of service and legalized the enlistment of minors without the permission of parent or guardian. In addition, Congress authorized taking up to 40,000 state troops into federal service for local defense and raising an additional 40,000 volunteers for service against Canada. To boost naval recruiting, the administration adopted more incentives: a bounty (up to $30), a 25 percent boost in pay, and an advance in pay.

In the hope of stabilizing the nation's finances, Congress adopted a new round of internal taxes and considered re-establishing the national bank. To curtail widespread trade with the enemy, Congress adopted a new enemy trade act that gave government officials sweeping powers to search for and seize trade goods.

It's hard to say how effective these measures were. Although they represented a reasonable attempt to deal with the crisis, the war ended before they could be given a fair test. Moreover, some of the measures drove the Federalists to still greater opposition and increased their willingness to openly obstruct the war effort.

150 | How did Federalists obstruct the war effort?

In Congress they voted as a bloc on all war-related legislation during the war. Although they supported the navy and coastal fortifications (which they considered long-term defensive measures), they voted against all bills to raise men or money or to promote privateering. In New England, Federalists went further. They openly wrote, spoke, and preached against the war, they discouraged enlistments in the army and subscriptions to the war loans, and on occasion they even withheld their state militias from federal service.

151 | Did Federalists consider supporting the war in 1814?

Yes, they did, but in the end nothing came of it. There was considerable talk among Federalists in the middle and southern states about ending their opposition because the character of the war seemed to have changed, from a war of conquest to a war to protect American territory. But New England Federalists remained obstinate, arguing that nothing had really changed, that Canada was still in the administration's cross hairs, and that the best way to end the war was to continue opposing it.

The actions of the Republican administration in Washington seemed to confirm New England's view. Secretary of War James Monroe laid out a plan for raising a large army in 1815 by resorting to conscription and launching yet another bid to conquer Canada. Also, despite public pressure to take some Federalists into the cabinet in order to forge a united front against the enemy, the administration refused to do so. According to one Federalist, Madison thought it would be "a passport to the Presidency" if he acknowledged the talents of any Federalist by taking him into the cabinet.[42] Finally, by the end of the year the news from Europe suggested that the British were willing to end the war on reasonable terms, and this further dampened any enthusiasm that Federalists might have mustered for the war.

Facing an unyielding administration and a conciliatory enemy, Federalists in the middle and southern states once again cast their lot with New England. In the last months of the war, Federalists continued to present a united front against the administration and its war policies. Moreover, in New England there was growing talk of making a separate peace and perhaps even leaving the Union. "The cloud arising in the East," warned a New Jersey Federalist, "was black, alarming, [and] portentous."[43] The climax of this sectional opposition was the Hartford Convention.

152 | What was the Hartford Convention?

It was a regional conference convened by New England Federalists to air their grievances against the Republican administration in Washington and its policies, particularly the war. The meeting was held in Hartford, Connecticut, from December 15, 1814, to January 5, 1815, and was attended by twenty-six delegates who represented Massachusetts, Connecticut, Rhode Island, and several counties in New Hampshire and Vermont. Although there was a lot of talk in New England of pulling out of the Union, there was no real secessionist movement in the region, and at Hartford the moderates remained firmly in control.

This triumph of moderation was clear in the report of the convention, which was made public on January 6, 1815. More than half of it was devoted to war-related issues: congressional bills to raise an army by conscription or authorize the enlistment of minors without the consent of parent or guardian; a dispute with the federal government over the control and deployment of the militia; and the failure of Washington to provide for the defense of the region or to give the states the money they needed to look after their own defense. The report recommended that the states nullify any unconstitutional military laws and that they be permitted to preempt federal tax revenue collected within their jurisdiction to defray the cost of local defense measures.

The report also proposed seven constitutional amendments to prevent a recurrence of those Republican policies that Federalists considered most inimical to New England in particular and the

Union in general. These called for: (1) requiring a two-thirds vote in Congress to declare war, interdict commerce with a foreign nation, or admit new states to the Union; (2) a sixty-day limit on embargoes; (3) the elimination of the clause that counted three-fifths of slaves in apportioning seats in the House of Representatives; (4) a ban against naturalized citizens holding federal office; and (5) a provision that would limit presidents to a single term and prohibit any state from providing the president twice in succession.

153 | Were the Hartford Convention proposals adopted?

For the most part, no. Connecticut and Massachusetts adopted laws nullifying the federal minor enlistment law, but the former acted just before the war ended, and the latter waited until the conflict was over and recruiting had been suspended. The same two states also sent delegates to Washington to discuss the preemption of federal funds, and the constitutional amendments were introduced in both houses of Congress. But nothing came of these proposals. The New England Federalists had neither the votes nor the influence to get their way, and the end of the war killed what little chance they had.

154 | Why did the British target the Gulf Coast in 1814–1815?

A campaign against the Gulf Coast, with New Orleans as the main objective, had been proposed as early as November 1812 by Admiral Sir John Borlase Warren to force the redeployment of American troops from the north and thus reduce the pressure on Canada. But this proposal did not become part of British strategy until 1814, and by then the British were more interested in seizing territory that might be used as a bargaining chip in the peace negotiations.

Vice Admiral Sir Alexander Cochrane had replaced Warren and was charged with implementing the plan. Initially, Cochrane planned to rely heavily on Creek Indians, runaway slaves, and dissident Spaniards, but the arrival of a large army, which ultimately came under the command of General Edward Pakenham, the Duke of Wellington's brother-in-law, made this unnecessary.

In May 1814, the British landed a small force on the Apalachicola River in Spanish Florida and distributed arms to the Indians there. The following August, another small British force, acting with the blessing of local Spanish officials, occupied Pensacola. From here, the British in September launched an attack against Fort Bowyer, which protected the approaches to Mobile Bay. The attack failed because the assaulting force was too small, and in the shallow waters of the bay the British flagship *Hermes* (22 guns) ran aground and had to be destroyed.

Andrew Jackson, who was now a major general in the regular army and responsible for the defense of the Gulf Coast, drove the British out of Pensacola in November, then hastily pulled together a motley collection of regulars, volunteers, militia, and Indians to resist the large British force that was known to be en route to New Orleans. The British landed about eighty miles south of New Orleans in December 1814 and, after disposing of a flotilla of U.S. gunboats in the Battle of Lake Borgne on the fourteenth, worked their way to Jacques Villeré's plantation about eight miles south of New Orleans. Three inconclusive engagements followed—the Battle of Villeré's Plantation, also known as the Night Engagement (on December 23); the British Reconnaissance in Force (on December 28); and the Battle of Rodrigues Canal, also called the Artillery Duel (on January 1)—before the main Battle of New Orleans was fought on January 8.

155 | What happened in the Battle of New Orleans?

Jackson had established a defensive line south of New Orleans that extended from the Mississippi River in the west to an impenetrable cypress swamp in the east. The line was anchored by eight powerful artillery batteries and defended by around 5,000 troops. Jackson also positioned a militia force on the west bank of the river. The British launched one prong of their attack against those citizen soldiers, but though successful, that attack came too late to affect the outcome on the east bank.

Pakenham launched a frontal assault against Jackson's main line with about 5,000 men. When the first elements were within 500 yards, Jackson's artillery opened fire. Using mostly grapeshot and canister, the heavy guns tore large holes in the advancing lines, and when the British got closer, they had to contend with small arms fire from rifles and muskets. Only one British column, by the river, got close enough to penetrate Jackson's line, but these men were forced back by heavy fire.

The effect of the American fire was devastating. A British veteran of the Napoleonic Wars described it as "the most murderous I ever beheld before or since."[44] After little more than half an hour, the British withdrew with staggering losses—around 1,500 killed or wounded and another 500 captured. Jackson's own losses, by contrast, were only seventy, and only thirteen of those were on the east side of the river. The lopsided figures suggested a decisive American victory in the biggest and bloodiest battle of the war.

156 | What was the impact of Jackson's victory at New Orleans?

Enormous. Most Americans saw it as a defining moment—the battle that gave them victory in the war. Jackson himself emerged

This depiction of the Battle of New Orleans shows how exposed the advancing British troops were, particularly to deadly canister and grapeshot from the artillery batteries that anchored Jackson's line. (Drawing by A. Hotzy. Lithograph by P. S. Duval. United States Military Magazine, *1841.)*

from the war as an outsized hero and ultimately became president. Ironically he was honored everywhere except in New Orleans. On December 16, Jackson had proclaimed martial law in New Orleans to control the movement of people—and intelligence—in and out of the city, but he was slow to release his iron grip even after the British had been defeated. Although reports of peace reached the Gulf Coast as early as February 19, Jackson refused to lift martial law until he had received official news nearly a month later, on March 13. In the meantime, he had jailed a state legislator who had written a newspaper article complaining about martial law as well as a federal judge who had ordered the legislator released. Later, Jackson was hauled into the same court and fined $1,000 for contempt (a fine that Congress refunded, with interest, many years later when the aging hero had fallen on hard times). When the Louisiana legislature adopted resolutions thanking those who had saved the city, Jackson's name was nowhere to be found.

157 | Did the British leave the Gulf Coast after the Battle of New Orleans?

No. Instead of withdrawing after their defeat at New Orleans, the British force on the Gulf Coast launched a lengthy bombardment of Fort St. Philip on the Mississippi River, then captured Fort Bowyer, which protected Mobile. Fort St. Philip was erected on a sharp bend on the Mississippi River sixty-five miles south of New Orleans. Because of the currents, ships sailing upriver moved slowly through the bend and thus presented easy targets for the fort's batteries. By early 1815, the fort had become a formidable post defended by 400 men under the command of Major Walter H. Overton.

To open the river to Royal warships, a British squadron commenced bombarding Fort St. Philip on January 9 and continued for nine days. The British reportedly expended 20,000 pounds of powder and seventy tons of shot and shell but without subduing the fort. Like the bombardment of Fort McHenry four months earlier, this showed the limits of naval power against well-constructed and heavily armed coastal fortifications.

The British had targeted Fort Bowyer without success the previous September, but in February 1815 they returned in much greater strength. Some 5,000 British troops landed and surrounded the fort on three sides. Supported by artillery that was brought within a hundred yards of the fort, the British opened fire. With only 375 men at his disposal, Major William Lawrence could offer only token resistance before surrendering on February 11. Before the British could occupy Mobile, however, news of peace arrived.

158 | Did the war at sea continue in 1815?

Yes, it did. American warships were still able to slip out to sea on occasion, and there were two naval engagements. In the first, the United States lost the heavy frigate *President,* and in the second the *Constitution* defeated two British warships.

Captain Stephen Decatur, who had taken command of the *President* (carrying 53 guns), escaped from New York Harbor in a severe snow storm on January 14. His aim was to sail to the Strait of Malacca and attack the East India Company's rich China fleet. But shortly after leaving port, the *President* ran aground. Although Decatur managed to free his ship, she evidently had lost some of her sailing qualities.

The following day, Decatur found himself pursued by the *Endymion* (47 guns), commanded by Captain Henry Hope, and several other British ships. *Endymion* was a fast ship and she was superbly handled. Hope caught up with the *President,* stayed to her starboard, and pummeled her at close range. The American ship could not escape, nor, with the other British ships nearby, could Decatur bring her around to take advantage of her superior firepower. Eventually, the two ships exchanged broadsides, after which the *Endymion* disengaged, but by then the *President* had sustained so much damage that Decatur had to surrender. For the British, this was a noteworthy victory, the only time during the war that they defeated a heavy American frigate.

Unlike the *President,* the *Constitution* (mounting 52 guns) continued her run of good luck. Now under the command of Captain

Charles Stewart, the *Constitution* sailed from Boston at the end of December 1814. By February 20 she was near the Madeira Islands off the coast of Africa. There she encountered two Royal Navy ships, the *Cyane* (33 guns), commanded by Captain Gordon Falcon, and the 21-gun *Levant*, under Captain George Douglas.

Although the British ships might have fled from such a powerful foe, they chose instead to engage her. In a masterful display of seamanship and gunnery, Captain Stewart pounded both into submission. When a British squadron appeared, Stewart had to abandon his prizes, although the prize crew on the *Cyane* still managed to steer her into an American port. Stewart was able to get the *Constitution* back to port as well. The *Constitution*'s final cruise kept her perfect record intact, and "Old Ironsides" emerged from the war as the nation's most-celebrated warship.

159 | When did peace negotiations begin?

The first round of talks actually began within a week of the declaration of war. President Madison, hoping that the declaration of war would by itself win concessions from the British, sent peace feelers through various channels. "The sword was scarcely out of the scabbard," Madison told the American people, "before the enemy was apprized of the reasonable terms on which it would be resheathed."[45]

The United States demanded an end to the Orders-in-Council and impressment. As it happened, the British announced the repeal of the Orders on June 23, just five days after the declaration of war. That might have forestalled war had it come earlier, but it was too late. The news did not reach Washington until August 13, and the Republican administration refused to agree to peace unless the British also gave up impressment. The British refused to budge on this issue, and the peace negotiations of 1812 came to naught.

160 | Why did Russia offer to mediate an end to the war?

On March 8, 1813, Russia hoped to restore peace by offering its services as mediator. The war had ended American trade to Baltic ports, and the Russians were eager to restore this trade to gain access to tropical commodities that American merchants customarily brought them. In addition, the Russians had no desire to see their ally against Napoleonic France fritter away resources on an American war.

The Americans quickly accepted because already the war was going badly for them, but the British declined because they had no wish to take part in any negotiations sponsored by an inland power that was likely to favor the American definition of neutral rights.

161 | When and where did the peace negotiations take place?

Having rejected the Russian offer, the British in November 1813 countered by offering direct negotiations to the United States, though they made it clear that they would not surrender any of their maritime rights. The United States quickly accepted, and negotiations took place from August 8 to December 24, 1814, in Ghent, located in present-day Belgium.

162 | Who represented each side in the negotiations?

The United States was represented by a five-man delegation. Headed by future president John Quincy Adams, it included former speaker of the house Henry Clay, former secretary of the treasury Albert Gallatin, Federalist senator James A. Bayard, and a minor diplomatic functionary named Jonathan Russell. It was an able and distinguished group. The British, by contrast, reserved their top diplomats for the Congress of Vienna, which was scheduled to meet that fall to forge a general peace for Europe. London sent a three-man team to Ghent that was far less distinguished than the American delegation. It was headed by a veteran naval officer, Admiral Sir James Gambier, and included William Adams, an Admiralty lawyer, and Henry Goulburn, an undersecretary in the Colonial Office. Gallatin, Adams, and Clay dominated the American delegation, Goulburn the British delegation.

163 | What were the initial terms for peace?

By the time the negotiations got under way, the United States had dropped its demand for an end to impressment and was willing to restore peace on the basis of the *status quo ante bellum*—the state of affairs that existed before the war. The British, however, were now in the driver's seat militarily and presented their own terms, which were designed mainly to protect their subjects in Canada and their native allies from future American aggression.

The British demanded: (1) the creation of a permanent Indian reservation in the Old Northwest; (2) territorial concessions in what is today northern Minnesota to give their fur traders direct access to the Mississippi River, and in northern Maine so that they could establish a direct land route from Quebec to Halifax; (3) the removal of all American warships and forts from the Great Lakes; and (4) an end to American fishing privileges in British North American waters.

164 | What was the reaction to the British demands?

The American delegates were stunned to learn that the United States could not make peace without paying a price. When they

The Treaty of Ghent was signed on December 24, 1814. Pictured here are the two delegation heads, Lord Gambier (1756–1833) on the left and John Quincy Adams (1767–1848), shaking hands. They are flanked by members of their respective delegations. (Lithograph of painting by A. Forestier. Library and Archives of Canada.)

rejected those terms, the British retreated to an offer of *uti possidetis,* which meant that each side would keep whatever territory it held at the end of the war. This would have transferred eastern Maine and forts Mackinac and Niagara to Great Britain and the strip of territory in western Upper Canada that includes Fort Amherstburg to the United States. When the United States also rejected that offer, the British agreed to the American demand to return to the *status quo ante bellum.*

165 | When was the peace treaty signed?

On December 24, 1814. It is commonly called the Treaty of Ghent but is also known as the Peace of Christmas Eve.

166 | Did signing the Treaty of Ghent end the War of 1812?

No. The British feared that the U.S. government might demand changes in the agreement before ratifying, and that this would put them in a difficult position if they had already agreed to a suspension of hostilities. The British insisted on a clause that provided for ending the war only after both sides had ratified the treaty.

The British ratified on December 27, 1814, but the treaty did not reach the United States until February 1815. The U.S. Senate approved it by a unanimous vote on February 16, and later that day President Madison affixed his own signature, thus completing the ratification process. This ended the war, and both nations immediately sent out orders suspending all military operations.

167 | Were there any military engagements after the peace treaty was ratified?

Yes, but these were minor skirmishes, mostly on the high seas, because it took time for the news of peace to spread. The treaty acknowledged this communication lag by providing that any prizes taken at sea within twelve to 120 days of ratification (depending on how remote the waters were) did not have to be restored.

The last military engagement of the war took place in the Indian Ocean on June 30, 1815. The U.S. Sloop *Peacock*, mounting 22 guns and commanded by Master Commandant Lewis Warrington, ordered the East India cruiser *Nautilus*, 14 guns, commanded by Lieutenant Charles Boyce, to strike its colors. When Boyce refused, claiming that the war was over, Warrington opened fire. In this one-sided engagement, the British ship sustained fifteen casualties, one of whom was Boyce, who lost a leg.

168 | What was the Dartmoor Massacre?

This was a violent confrontation that took place nearly two months after the war was over at a prison housing 6,500 American prisoners of war in Great Britain. When a dispute arose over who ought to pay for repatriating the Americans, their return to the United States was delayed. The prisoners, whose living conditions were miserable, became increasingly restive, and tensions rose. On April 6, 1815, when the Americans became unruly, the prison's governor entered the prison at the head of a column of local militia and opened fire, killing six and wounding sixty more.

169 | Did Britain's Indian allies continue the war against the United States?

Yes, at least for a time most of them did. Assorted skirmishes broke out for many months after the ratification of the peace treaty, most notably the Battle of the Sinkhole on May 24 near St. Louis. Between July 18, 1815, and June 4, 1816, the United States signed peace treaties with the tribes that remained hostile. Even then some Creeks refused to come to terms but instead joined the Seminoles in Florida and offered resistance to the United States for many years thereafter.

CHAPTER SIX

The Legacy

170 | Who won the War of 1812?

Although the war ended in a stalemate on the battlefield, Great Britain and Canada were the big winners. The British made no concessions to the United States on the maritime issues that had caused the war, nor did they surrender any territory. Canada remained part of the British Empire instead of being forcibly annexed to the United States. It retained its identity and in 1867 became an independent nation.

171 | Who lost the war?

The biggest losers were the Indians on both sides of the border. On the U.S. side, they were forced to make peace on American terms and never again would have a reliable foreign ally to offset the growing power of the United States. Instead, they were forced to bow to the relentless pressure of American expansion, surrendering their territory and way of life and being confined to reservations. Indians on the Canadian side also lost because the British no longer cultivated them to offset American power. The process was slower than south of the border, but the end result was the same: a loss of territory and traditional mores and a new way of life on reservations.

For the United States, the outcome of the war was more ambiguous. The new nation managed to beat back the British invasion in 1814–15 and avoid making any concessions in the peace treaty, and it enjoyed a new confidence in itself and a heightened respect abroad. But in a fundamental way it had lost the war, because it failed to achieve its war aims. It won no concessions on the maritime issues, which were not even mentioned in the Treaty of Ghent, nor did it succeed in conquering Canada. Ironically, the one piece of territory the United States acquired during the war was a strip of West Florida it seized from neutral Spain in 1813.

172 | Who won the peace?

Undoubtedly, the United States did. Even though the end of the war in Europe gave Britain a huge military and naval advantage on this side of the Atlantic, the United States successfully resisted its demands for concessions. The provision in the peace treaty for a return to the *status quo ante bellum* was a great triumph for the fledgling nation. In a broad sense, the Treaty of Ghent confirmed American independence.

173 | What were the most significant battles?

Because the war had several theaters of operations, there were many. For the United States, the most significant battle in 1812 was the *Constitution*'s duel with the *Guerrière*, because it gave a boost to sagging American morale and launched the illustrious career of "Old Ironsides." In 1813 the battles of Lake Erie and the Thames destroyed Tecumseh's confederacy and secured the Old Northwest. In 1814 the battles of Chippawa and Lundy's Lane established the reputation of the U.S. Army; the battle of Lake Champlain saved Upper New York from enemy occupation; North Point and the successful defense of Fort McHenry secured Baltimore and produced "The Star-Spangled Banner"; and the Battle of Horseshoe

Bend broke the power of the Creeks in the Old Southwest. In 1815 the key battle was at New Orleans, which saved the Crescent City from occupation, made Andrew Jackson's reputation, and shaped how Americans remembered the war.

For the British, the most significant battles in 1812 took place at Detroit and Queenston Heights, which preserved Upper Canada. The following year, 1813, Stoney Creek, Beaver Dams, and Fort Niagara consolidated Britain's hold on the Niagara front; Châteauguay and Crysler's Farm prevented an assault on Montreal; and the *Chesapeake-Shannon* duel restored the reputation of the Royal Navy. In 1814, most significant was the successful defense of Mackinac and the capture of the *Tigress* and *Scorpion* in Lake Huron because they preserved Britain's position in the Old Northwest, and the burning of Washington.

174 | How many people died in the war?

Records were poorly kept, so it is impossible to know with certainty. The United States lost 2,260 men in battle, but the total number of American soldiers, seamen, privateersmen, and civilians who died from combat wounds, disease, or accident as a direct result of the war was close to 20,000. Total British losses were probably around 10,000, and Indian losses perhaps 7,500. As a proportion of their population, the Indians were once more the biggest losers.

175 | How much did the war cost?

The direct cost to the United States (excluding property damage and lost economic opportunities) was $158 million. This includes $93 million in military and naval expenditures, $16 million for interest on the war loans, and $49 million to cover veterans' benefits. (The last veteran died in 1905 and the last pensioner, the daughter of a veteran, in 1946). On the $80 million that the Treasury borrowed to finance the war, it paid an average of 14 percent interest.

The cost to the British is more difficult to compute because so many of their forces, especially at sea, were actually waging two wars, one against France and the other against the United States, and the duties in these wars often overlapped. The British probably paid more than the United States to cover their costs at sea but less to cover their costs on land. In all likelihood, their total cost was similar to that of the United States. The cost to the Indians cannot be reckoned because they did not have a money-based economy, but in lost land alone the war cost them dearly.

176 | What was the economic impact of the war in the United States?

It depended on what you did for a living and where you lived. Many people in the middle and western states prospered from government contracts and manufacturing, which flourished during the war. New England, by contrast, suffered because foreign trade dried up, and even the coastal trade shrank. That affected merchants, seamen, and dockworkers as well as anyone else whose livelihood was tied to the sea. The South also suffered because commodities normally produced for export could not be shipped to foreign markets. The price of agricultural staples plummeted, and many farmers and planters sank deeper into debt. Soldiers suffered a great deal during the war, more from disease, the weather, and shortages of food and clothing than from enemy fire, but those who survived and completed their terms of enlistment were rewarded with sizeable cash and land bounties. Most people were probably better off before or after the war than during it.

177 | What impact did the war have on black people?

The war offered blacks on both sides an opportunity for military service. There had always been a large population of seafaring blacks in the Atlantic world, and the British and U.S. navies and privateers all had significant numbers of black seamen. Since most white seamen in the United States shunned gunboats, the crews in this service were often heavily black. The British army had black soldiers, and although the U.S. Army initially shunned black recruits, by the end of the war they were welcomed to meet manpower needs. Most state armies established in the last year of the war also welcomed black recruits. In a crisis, all hands, including free blacks and sometimes even slaves, were usually welcome. This was true at Baltimore in 1814 and at New Orleans in 1815.

The biggest winners among blacks were those slaves, probably around 4,000 in all, who fled to British camps and British warships in the Chesapeake and elsewhere along the Atlantic or Gulf Coast. Close to 900 served in a special corps of Colonial Marines organized by the Royal Navy. They saw considerable action, especially in the Chesapeake, where they served as scouts, provided intelligence, and took part in a number of raids. They proved steady in battle because they could not risk capture. After the war, all the runaways who had taken refuge with the British were resettled in Canada, the West Indies, and other parts of the British Empire. For them, the War of 1812 truly was a war of independence. Even though many suffered in their new homes, they did so as freedmen.

178 | What impact did the war have on women?

Women in this war, as in most wars, played an important role behind the scenes. They managed families and sometimes businesses and farms for men who were away, and they nursed the injured and wounded who returned home. Women also produced ammunition because it was difficult to hire men for that kind of work at the prevailing wage.

Women could also be found with armies in the field. Some were the wives of soldiers or of civilians attached to the army. Others, on their own, made a living sewing, cooking, or providing other services to the soldiers. Women were employed in the medical corps, hauled food and water to men in the front lines, occasionally helped prepare defenses, and even took part in battles. Fanny Doyle was the wife of an American artillery private who was captured in the Battle of Queenston Heights. Five weeks later, on November 21, 1812, Betsy Doyle Doyle took part in a fierce artillery duel between Fort George and Fort Niagara. According to Lieutenant Colonel George McFeely, she showed "extraordinary bravery" in the engagement. "During the most tremendous cannonading I have ever seen, she attended the six-pounder on the [Fort Niagara] mess-house [roof] with red hot shot, and showed fortitude equal to the Maid of Orleans [Joan of Arc]."[46]

Although the war did not change the status of women, Dolley Madison and Laura Secord were ultimately recognized for their contributions to the war effort and emerged as genuine heroes.

179 | How effective was President Madison as the U.S. war leader?

Not very. He was probably the weakest wartime president in American history. Shy and introspective, Madison had a first-class mind but was unsuited to provide the sort of inspired leadership needed in wartime. He allowed back-biting, feuding, and disloyalty in his cabinet, failed to develop an effective strategy for winning the war, was slow to discipline uncooperative generals or to remove weak ones, and was unable to control an often fractious Congress. Unlike some wartime presidents, Madison showed a commendable regard for the civil rights of those who opposed him or the war, but the flip side of that regard was an unwillingness to exercise the sort of arbitrary power that is sometimes needed to push war to a successful conclusion.

180 | How effective was Sir George Prevost as the Canadian war leader?

Much more so. Although he did not shine as a field commander, especially when charged with undertaking offensive operations, Prevost did a fine job in the first two years of the war, husbanding his limited resources to beat back the American invasion. More than anyone else in this war, Sir George was the savior of Canada. Unfortunately, because of his failures in the field, he is not remembered this way, and he died before he could make a case for himself in a court-martial or in the court of public opinion.

181 | Was this a second war of independence for the United States?

Not in any real sense. The British maritime practices that caused the war infringed upon American rights but were a direct outgrowth of the war in Europe and would end when that war ended. The British had no real designs on American sovereignty, no desire to roll back the Declaration of Independence or to recolonize the United States. Even when the British took the offensive in 1814, their campaigns were not designed to undermine American independence but to win territory that might be used to bargain for greater security for their North American provinces and their Indian allies. Although in a broad sense the war confirmed American independence, that independence was never truly at risk.

182 | What was the legacy of the war for the United States?

By celebrating the naval victories on the high seas and inland lakes and the military triumphs at the Thames, Baltimore, and New Orleans, Americans convinced themselves that they had won the war. They had preserved the nation from conquest by decisively defeating the Mistress of the Seas and the conqueror of Napoleon. Indeed, they had defeated "the conquerors of the conquerors of Europe." The war fostered a robust nationalism and generated a buoyant self-confidence at home while earning greater respect abroad.

The war also produced a new generation of military leaders, headed by Jacob Brown and Winfield Scott, as well as a new set of naval leaders such as Oliver Hazard Perry and Thomas Macdonough, who demonstrated a talent for command and dominated the military establishment until mid-century and beyond. A new generation of statesmen also emerged from the war. Men like James Monroe, John Quincy Adams, Henry Clay, and John C. Calhoun seized control of the nation's destiny and left their mark on the developing republic in the postwar era. Above all, there was Andrew Jackson, both a military and civilian leader, who became the great symbol for the postwar era, epitomizing its full-bodied patriotism, its raw, frontier democracy, and its unshakable commitment to territorial expansion.

The United States also emerged from the war with several powerful new symbols that shaped the cultural landscape and helped Americans better understand who they were. There was the Fort McHenry flag and "The Star-Spangled Banner" as well as

Most people on both sides of the Atlantic thought that the two English-speaking nations would surely come to blows again, but this contemporary image, with symbolic representatives of the two nations joining hands, was a more accurate prediction of the future. (Ink and watercolor by John Rubens Smith. Library of Congress.)

"Old Ironsides" and the trophy ship *Macedonian* to remind Americans of their success in the war. Uncle Sam made his first appearance as a symbol for the U.S. government, and the Kentucky Rifle, a uniquely American weapon, earned a reputation (although much inflated) for defeating the British, especially at New Orleans. Finally, there were the sayings—"We have met the enemy and they are ours" and "Don't give up the ship"—that entered the lexicon of American patriotism. These symbols and sayings became part of the nation's cultural heritage. Although the War of 1812 was not truly a second war of independence, it nonetheless helped Americans forge a national identity.

183 | What was the legacy for Canada?

The war also looms large in Canadian history, although Canadians were slower than Americans to appreciate its significance. The war's immediate effect was to strengthen Canadian ties to the British Empire. Not until 1867 did the disparate provinces that made up British North America become the Dominion of Canada, and only many years later did Canadians realize that the American war had been a crucial benchmark in their national development.

The war was the closest thing that Canadians had to a civil war or a war of independence. It was like a civil war in that Canadians had to overcome defeatism and collaboration in order to prevail, and it resembled a war of independence in that victory was essential to avoid being swallowed up by the United States. More broadly, the war fostered the unity, patriotism, and identity that defined the nation that later emerged.

In time, Canadians embraced the heroes of the war, and the great 1812 figures—Isaac Brock, Charles de Salaberry, Tecumseh, and Laura Secord—became part of the Canadian pantheon. These iconic figures, in turn, helped Canadians further define who they were and what their nation was all about.

184 | What was the legacy for Great Britain?

Even though the War of 1812 was always overshadowed in the public memory by the Napoleonic Wars and thus quickly forgotten, the conflict produced a few revered British icons, most notably Captain Philip Broke and the *Shannon*, which had vanquished the U.S. Frigate *Chesapeake* in such short order in 1813. Nor were the lessons of the war lost on British leaders. For the balance of the nineteenth century and beyond, the British recognized that it was in their interest to cultivate the young republic, even if sometimes that meant sacrificing important interests in Canada or other provinces in the British Empire.

The road to friendship in Anglo-American relations was rocky, but soaring trade and a shared commitment to democracy, the rule of law, and free markets ultimately brought the two English-speaking nations together. A series of treaties along the way smoothed the road: a modest commercial agreement in 1815, the landmark Rush-Bagot Agreement in 1817 that set the stage for demilitarizing the entire northern border, and the Treaty of Washington in 1871, which liquidated most remaining problems. The lessons of 1812 propelled both nations to seek an accommodation, and by 1900 the traditional antagonism had been replaced by a genuine Anglo-American accord. The experience of two world wars and a cold war later cemented that accord into the close and lasting partnership that persists to this day.

185 | What was the legacy for Indians?

For Indians the War of 1812 was an important watershed.

Although the peace treaty bound the United States to restore to the Indians all the rights and territory that they had enjoyed as of 1811, this clause was a dead letter. It was not simply that the tribes in the Old Northwest had to accept whatever terms were offered or that the Creeks in the Old Southwest were stripped of so much land. It was that native tribes everywhere no longer had any leverage in their negotiations with the United States because they had forever lost the support of the European allies they had once counted upon. Although the demographic clock was already ticking against indigenous people, the War of 1812 ended their role as significant players in North America and thus hurried their tragic descent into reservation life. Never again would the United States be cowed by the war whoop, never again would the native population play a central role in shaping the future of North America. The War of 1812 had put an end to that.

186 | When did the war of 1812 become the War of 1812?

At the time, contemporaries called the conflict simply "the war." Some Federalists referred to it as "Mr. Madison's War," but that phrase never caught on. After the conflict ended, it was referred to as "the recent war," "the late war," or "the late war with Great Britain." Although the phrase "War of 1812" had been used as early as 1812, this term did not come into general usage until the 1830s and did not become universal until the 1850s. By then, the Mexican War (1846–48) had been fought, and it was now necessary to distinguish between "late" wars. Shortly thereafter, the Civil War erupted, a conflict of such monumental importance that it swept the two preceding wars into the deep recesses of the public memory.

187 | Why should we remember this war today?

Although the War of 1812 hardly ranks with the American Revolution, the Civil War, or the world wars of the twentieth century as a truly historic conflict, it nevertheless deserves to be remembered because it was so important in shaping the transatlantic community. Arguably, it forged two nations in North America and defined how Great Britain—the dominant European power and Mistress of the Seas—would relate to them. Although many people on both sides of the Atlantic assumed that the Peace of Ghent would be transitory and that eventually there would be another Anglo-American war, such was not the case. The War of 1812 had generated just enough respect on both sides to make each nation reluctant to repeat it. Had that not been the case, the character of the Pax Britannia in the nineteenth century might have been different, and there might not have been such a seamless transition to the Pax Americana in the twentieth.

Chronology

The following chronology presents the dates for all events mentioned in the text. The more important military and diplomatic events are in **bold** type.

Abbreviations:

US = United States
GB = Great Britain

Capt = Captain
BG = Brigadier general
MG = Major general

HM = His Majesty's
(n) = Number of guns an armed ship carried

Current US states and Canadian provinces where events took place are identified by their two-letter postal codes.

1801

March 4: Thomas Jefferson inaugurated as president

1806–1807

France issues Continental Decrees

1807–1809

GB issues Orders-in-Council

1807

June 22: *Chesapeake* affair
December 22: US adopts embargo

1808–1809

British spy John Henry gathers intelligence in New England

1809

March 4: James Madison inaugurated as president

1811

May 16: *Little Belt* affair
October 21: Sir George Prevost appointed captain-general and
governor-in-chief of Canada
November 7: Battle of Tippecanoe (IN)
November 12: US and GB settle *Chesapeake* affair
Dec. 24–April 10: US enacts war preparations

1812

March 9: President Madison submits papers of British spy John Henry
to Congress
June 1: President Madison sends war message to US Congress
4: House of Representatives adopts war bill
5: Mob assaults Federalist editor in Savannah (GA)
8: Earl of Liverpool becomes prime minister of GB
16: GB announces interest in suspending Orders-in-Council
17: Senate adopts war bill
18: Madison signs war bill into law (War of 1812 begins)

18–26: US sends out peace feelers

June 22–Aug. 4: Baltimore Riots (MD)

June 23: France invades Russia

23: GB repeals Orders-in-Council

July 1: US doubles customs duties

6: US adopts first enemy trade law

11: GB restores deserters taken in *Chesapeake* affair in Boston Harbor (MA)

12: US invades Canada across Detroit River (MI/ON)

16–19: US Frigate *Constitution* (55) outruns British squadron

17: GB captures Fort Mackinac (MI)

28: Mob assaults Federalist editor in Norristown (PA)

30: News of war reaches London (GB)

August 13: News of repeal of Orders-in-Council reaches Washington (DC)

15: Fort Dearborn Massacre (IL)

16: GB captures Detroit (MI)

19: US Frigate *Constitution* (55) defeats HM Ship *Guerrière* (49)

Sept.–Nov.: Elections of 1812

Fall: GB blockades South Atlantic Coast (SC/GA)

October 13: Battle of Queenston Heights (ON); MG Isaac Brock killed

13: GB authorizes general reprisals against US

Oct. 19–Dec. 14: France retreats from Russia

25: US Frigate *United States* (56) captures HM Ship *Macedonian* (49)

November 19: US invades Lower Canada (NY/QC)

20: Battle of Lacolle Mill (QC)

December 17–18: Battle of Mississinewa (IN)

29: US Frigate *Constitution* (54) defeats HM Ship *Java* (49)

1813

January 18: First engagement at Frenchtown (MI)

 22: **Battle of Frenchtown (MI)**

 23: **River Raisin Massacre (MI)**

February 6: **GB proclaims blockade of Delaware and Chesapeake bays**

 9: Red Sticks raid frontier settlement (KY)

March 8: Russia offers to mediate end to War of 1812

 11: US accepts Russia's mediation offer

April 15: US occupies part of Spanish West Florida (AL/MS)

 27: **US captures York (ON);** BG Zebulon Pike killed

 29: GB burns Frenchtown (MD)

 29: GB attacks Fort Defiance/Elkton (MD)

May 1–9: **First Siege of Fort Meigs (OH)**

 3: GB burns Havre de Grace (MD)

 3: GB destroys Principio Ironworks (MD)

 5: Surrender of Charlestown (MD)

 6: GB burns Fredericktown (MD)

 6: GB burns Georgetown (MD)

 26: **GB proclaims blockade of major ports in middle and southern states**

 27: **US captures Fort George (ON)**

 29: **Battle of Sackets Harbor (NY)**

June 1: HM Ship *Shannon* (52) defeats US Frigate *Chesapeake* (50)

 3: GB captures US Sloop *Eagle* (11) and US Sloop *Growler* (11) in Richelieu River (QC)

 5–6: **Battle of Stoney Creek (ON)**

 22: **Battle of Craney Island (VA)**

 22–23: Laura Secord's trek (ON)

 24: **Battle of Beaver Dams (ON)**

 26: GB attacks Hampton (VA)

July 5: GB rejects Russian mediation offer

 21–28: Second siege of Fort Meigs (OH)

July 24–Aug. 2: US adopts internal taxes

July 27: Battle of Burnt Corn (AL)

August 1–2: Battle of Fort Stephenson (OH)

8: US Schooner *Hamilton* (9) and US Schooner *Scourge* (10) sink in Lake Ontario

10: GB attacks St. Michaels (MD)

13: GB attacks Queenstown (MD)

26: GB attacks St. Michaels (MD)

30: Fort Mims Massacre (AL)

September 10: Battle of Lake Erie

18: GB evacuates Fort Detroit (MI)

28: "Burlington Races" on Lake Ontario

October 5: Battle of the Thames/Moraviantown (ON); Tecumseh killed

16–19: Battle of Leipzig/the Nations (Germany)

26: Battle of Châteauguay (QC)

November 4: GB offers US direct peace negotiations

11: Battle of Crysler's Farm (ON); BG Leonard Covington killed

November 16: GB proclaims blockade of remaining ports in middle and southern states

December 10: US evacuates Fort George and burns Newark (ON)

19: GB captures Fort Niagara (NY)

19–21: GB burns Lewiston, Youngstown, and Manchester (NY)

30: GB burns Buffalo and Black Rock (NY)

1814

March 14: US executes John Woods (AL)

26: US military court in Albany convicts BG William Hull of cowardice and neglect of duty (NY)

27: Battle of Horseshoe Bend (AL)

28: HM Ship *Phoebe* (46 or 53) and HM Sloop *Cherub* (26) defeat US Frigate *Essex* (46)

31: European allies enter Paris

April 7: GB attacks Pettipaug (CT)

11: Napoleon unconditionally abdicates throne

25: GB proclaims blockade of New England

28: Napoleon exiled to Elba in Mediterranean

May 5–6: Battle of Oswego (NY)

10: GB lands force on Apalachicola River (FL)

14–15: US raids Dover and nearby settlements (ON)

30: Battle of Sandy Creek (NY)

June 9–10: Rope walk from Sandy Creek to Sackets Harbor (NY)

27: US drops impressment demand

July 3: US captures Fort Erie (ON)

5: Battle of Chippawa (ON)

11: GB captures Moose Island (ME)

20: US destroys Fort St. Joseph (ON)

21: US raids Sault Ste. Marie (ON)

22: US and Miamis, Potawatomis, Ottawas, Shawnees, Kickapoos sign peace treaty at Greenville (OH)

25: Battle of Lundy's Lane (ON)

August: US public credit collapses

US banks suspend specie payments

3: Battle of Conjocta Creek (NY)

4: Battle of Fort Mackinac (MI)

8: Peace negotiations begin in Ghent (Belgium)

8–19: GB lays down initial peace terms

9: US signs peace treaty with Creeks at Fort Jackson (AL)

9–11: GB attacks Stonington (CT)

12: GB captures US Schooner *Somers* (2) and US Schooner *Ohio* (1) in Niagara River

14: GB occupies Pensacola (FL)

14: Battle of Nottawasaga (ON)

15: Battle of Fort Erie (ON)

22: US blows up its Chesapeake flotilla above Pig Point (MD)

24: **Battle of Bladensburg (MD)**

24–25: **GB burns Washington (DC)**

26: US abandons Fort Washington (MD)

27: Capt. Thomas Boyle of US privateer *Chasseur* (16) proclaims mock blockade of GB and Ireland

28: Nantucket declares neutrality (MA)

29: Surrender of Alexandria (VA)

31: Battle of Caulk's Field (MD)

31: GB invades New York

September 1–11: **GB occupies 100 miles of US coast from Eastport to Castine (ME)**

3: GB captures US Schooner *Tigress* (1) on Lake Huron

6: GB captures US Schooner *Scorpion* (2) on Lake Huron

11: Battle of Plattsburgh (NY)

11: **Battle of Lake Champlain;** Capt. George Downie killed

12: **Battle of North Point (MD);** MG Robert Ross killed

13–14: **GB bombards Fort McHenry (MD)**

14: Francis Scott Key writes "The Star-Spangled Banner"

15: Battle of Fort Bowyer (AL)

Sept. 15–June 9: Congress of Vienna meets (Austria)

September 17: US Sortie from Fort Erie (ON)

27: Boats from British squadron defeat US privateer *General Armstrong* (9)

October 8: US prohibits trade with Block Island (RI)

11: US privateer *Prince-de-Neufchatel* (17) defeats boats of HM Ship *Endymion* (47)

16: HM Ship *St. Lawrence* (104) sets sail on Lake Ontario

19: Battle of Cook's Mills/Lyon's Creek (ON)

21: GB offers peace on basis of *uti possidetis*

Oct. 22–Nov. 17: BG Duncan McArthur's Raid (ON)

November 5: US evacuates Fort Erie (ON)

6: Battle of Malcolm's Mills (ON)

7: US drives British from Pensacola (FL)

27: GB drops *uti possidetis*

December 14: Battle of Lake Borgne (LA)

Dec. 15–Jan. 5: Hartford Convention meets (CT)

Dec. 15–Feb. 27: US adopts internal taxes

December 16: MG Andrew Jackson proclaims martial law in New Orleans (LA)

23: Battle of Villeré's Plantation/Night Engagement at New Orleans (LA)

24: US and GB sign Treaty of Ghent

27: GB ratifies Treaty of Ghent

28: British Reconnaissance in Force at New Orleans (LA)

28: US Congress rejects conscription

1815

January 1: Battle of Rodriquez Canal/Artillery Duel at New Orleans (LA)

8: Battle of New Orleans (LA); MG Edward Pakenham and MG Samuel Gibbs killed

9–18: GB bombards Fort St. Philip (LA)

15: British squadron captures US Frigate *President* (53)

28: British military court in Montreal convicts MG Henry Procter of mismanaging Thames campaign (QC)

February 4: US adopts second enemy trade law

8–11: Siege and capture of Fort Bowyer (AL)

14: Treaty of Ghent reaches Washington (DC)

16: US Senate unanimously approves Treaty of Ghent

16: President Madison ratifies Treaty of Ghent (War of 1812 officially ends)

17: US Congress rejects national bank

20: US Frigate *Constitution* (52) defeats HM Ship *Cyane* (33) and HM Ship *Levant* (21)

21: US executes 6 militiamen in Mobile (AL)

March 13: MG Andrew Jackson lifts martial law in New Orleans (LA)

28: News of peace reaches London (GB)

31: MG Andrew Jackson convicted of contempt of court in New Orleans (LA)

April 6: Dartmoor Massacre (GB)

May 24: Battle of the Sinkhole (MO)

June 30: US Sloop *Peacock* (22) defeats East India cruiser *Nautilus* (14) (last battle of War of 1812)

July 18–20: US signs peace treaties with Potawatomis, Piankashaws, Teton Sioux, Sioux of the Lakes, Sioux of St. Peter's River, Yankton Sioux, and Omahas at Portage des Sioux (MO)

September 2–16: US signs peace treaties with Kickapoos, Chippewas, Ottawas, Potawatomis, Osages, Sauks, Foxes, and Iowas at Portage des Sioux (MO)

October 28: US signs peace treaty with Kansas at Portage des Sioux (MO)

1816

May 13: US signs peace treaty with Sauks at St. Louis (MO)

June 1–3: US signs peace treaties with Sioux of the Leaf, Sioux of the Broad Leaf, Sioux Who Shoot in the Pine Tops, and Winnebagoes at St. Louis (MO)

June 4: US signs peace treaty with Weas and Kickapoos at Fort Harrison (IN)

Further Reading

Many fine books and articles illuminate various dimensions of the War of 1812. For an assessment of the best, see Donald R. Hickey, "The Top 25 Books on the War of 1812," *War of 1812 Magazine* 2 (September 2007):online at <http: //www.napoleon-series.org/military/Warof1812/2007/Issue7/c_top25books.html>; and "The Top 25 Articles on the War of 1812," *War of 1812 Magazine* 3 (May 2008): online at <http: //www.napoleon-series.org/military/Warof1812/2008/Issue9/c_top25articles.html>.

The best account of the origins of the war, is in Reginald Horsman, *The Causes of the War of 1812* (Philadelphia: University of Pennsylvania Press, 1962). The best military history is probably still John K. Mahon, *The War of 1812* (1972; repr., New York, Da Capo Press, 1991), although the land operations are treated effectively and in detail by Robert S. Quimby, *The U.S. Army in the War of 1812: An Operational and Command Study,* 2 vols. (East Lansing: Michigan State University Press, 1997).

There is no good account of the war from the British perspective, but for a fine account from the Canadian perspective, see J. Mackay Hitsman, *The Incredible War of 1812: A Military History* (1965; updated by Donald E. Graves, Toronto: Robin Brass Studio, 1999).

For the role of Indians in the war, see Robert S. Allen, *His Majesty's Indian Allies: British Indian Policy in the Defence of Canada, 1774–1815* (Toronto: Dundurn Press, 1992); George F. G. Stanley, "The Indians in the War of 1812," *Canadian Historical Review* 31 (June 1950): 145–65; Carl Benn, *The Iroquois in the War of 1812* (Toronto: University of Toronto Press, 1998); and Frank L. Owsley Jr., *Struggle for the Gulf Borderlands: The Creek War and the Battle of New Orleans, 1812–1815* (1981; repr., Tuscaloosa: University of Alabama Press, 2000).

For the domestic and diplomatic history of the war from the

American perspective, see Donald R. Hickey, *The War of 1812: A Forgotten Conflict* (1989; Urbana: University of Illinois Press, 2012), and J. C. A. Stagg, *Mr. Madison's War: Politics, Diplomacy, and Warfare in the Early American Republic, 1783–1830* (Princeton: Princeton University Press, 1983). For an examination of the many misconceptions of the war on both sides, see Hickey's *Don't Give Up the Ship! Myths of the War of 1812* (Toronto: Robin Brass Studio and Urbana: University of Illinois Press, 2006).

There are several good regional studies, most notably Allan Everest, *The War of 1812 in the Champlain Valley* (Syracuse: Syracuse University Press, 1981); Walter Lord, *The Dawn's Early Light* (1972; repr., Baltimore: The Johns Hopkins University Press, 2012); and Christopher T. George, *Terror on the Chesapeake: The War of 1812 on the Bay* (Shippensburg, Pa.: White Mane Books, 2000). For the British attack on Washington and Baltimore, see Anthony S. Pitch, *The Burning of Washington: The British Invasion of 1814* (Annapolis, Md.: Naval Institute Press, 1998). For a fine social history of the war on the northern frontier, see Alan Taylor, *The Civil War of 1812: American Citizens, British Subjects, Irish Rebels, & Indian Allies* (New York: Alfred A. Knopf, 2010).

For those who would like to sample battlefield narrative and analysis at its best, any of the works by Canadian Donald E. Graves will do. See especially *Where Right and Glory Lead! The Battle of Lundy's Lane, 1814,* rev. ed. (Toronto: Robin Brass Studio, 1997), and *Field of Glory: The Battle of Crysler's Farm, 1813* (Toronto: Robin Brass Studio, 1999). For the important subject of wartime logistics, two works stand out: Jeffrey Kimball, "The Fog and Friction of Frontier War: The Role of Logistics in American Offensive Failure during the War of 1812," *Old Northwest* 5 (1979): 323–43; and Philip Lord Jr., "The Mohawk/Oneida Corridor: The Geography of Inland Navigation across New York," in David Curtis Skaggs and Larry L. Nelson, eds., *The Sixty Years' War for the Great Lakes, 1754–1814* (East Lansing: Michigan State University Press, 2001): 275–90.

Those interested in the imagery of the war might wish to consult

Donald R. Hickey and Connie D. Clark, *The Rockets' Red Glare: An Illustrated History of the War of 1812* (Baltimore: The Johns Hopkins University Press, 2011) and Victor Suthren, *The War of 1812* (Toronto: McClelland & Stewart, 2001).

References

1. Speech of Daniel Sheffey, January 3, 1812, in U.S. Congress, *Annals of Congress: Debates and Proceedings in the Congress of the United States, 1789–1824,* 42 vols. (Washington, D.C., 1834–56),12th Congress, 1st session, 623 (hereafter cited as *AC,* 12-1, and similarly for other sessions).

2. William E. Channing, quoted in William H. Channing, *Memoir of William Ellery Channing,* 3 vols. (London, 1848), 1:337.

3. Hartford *Connecticut Courant,* August 25, 1812.

4. Henry Clay to Thomas Bodley, December 18, 1813, in James F. Hopkins and Mary W. M. Hargreaves, eds., *The Papers of Henry Clay,* 11 vols. (Lexington: University of Kentucky Press , 1959–92), 1:842.

5. Winfield Scott, *Memoirs of Lieut.-General Scott,* 2 vols. (New York, 1864), 1:36.

6. Jefferson to William Duane, August 4, 1812, in Jefferson Papers, Library of Congress, Washington, D.C., microfilm edition, reel 46.

7. Speech of John Randolph, December 10, 1811, in *AC,* 12-1, 447.

8. Hull to secretary of war, August 26, 1812, in U.S. Department of War, Letters Received by the Secretary of War, Registered Series, 1801–1870, microfilm series M221, National Archives, Washington, D.C., reel 45.

9. Charles J. Ingersoll, *Historical Sketch of the Second War between the United States of America, and Great Britain,* 2 vols. (Philadelphia, 1845–49), 1:102.

10. Brock to brothers, September 3, 1812, in Frederick B. Tupper, *The Life and Correspondence of Major-General Sir Isaac Brock, K.B.,* 2nd ed. (London, 1847), 285.

11. Moses Smith, *Naval Scenes in the Last War* (Boston, 1846), 33.

12. Letter of "Faber," March 5, 1813, in *Naval Chronicle,* 29 (January–June, 1813), 198.

13. Philadelphia *Aurora,* October 29, 1812.

14. Bennington [Vermont] *News-Letter,* December 23, 1812.

15. Perry to Harrison, September 10, 1813, in Benson J. Lossing Jr., *The*

Pictorial Field-Book of the War of 1812 (New York, 1868), 530. Perry actually captured two ships, *two* schooners, *one* brig, and a sloop.

16. Quoted in Thomas D. Clark, "Kentucky in the Northwest Campaign," in Philip P. Mason, ed., *After Tippecanoe: Some Aspects of the War of 1812* (East Lansing: Michigan State University Press, 2011), 94.

17. James F. Cooper, ed., *Ned Myers; or, A Life before the Mast* (Annapolis, Md.: Naval Institute Press, 1989), 56.

18. Letter of Albany *Argus*, December 26, 1813, reprinted in Washington (D.C.) *Universal Gazette*, January 1, 1814.

19. Tompkins to John Armstrong, January 2, 1814, in Hugh Hastings, ed., *Public Papers of Daniel D. Tompkins, Governor of New York, 1807–1817*, 3 vols. (New York, 1898–1902), 3:408.

20. John Reid and John Eaton, *The Life of Andrew Jackson* (Philadelphia, 1817), 143.

21. Jackson to Rachel Jackson, April 1, 1814, in Jackson Papers, Library of Congress, Washington, DC, microfilm edition, reel 9.

22. John Lovett to Joseph Alexander, May 18, 1813, in Catharina V. R. Bonney, *A Legacy of Historical Gleanings*, 2 vols. (Albany, N.Y., 1875), 1:297.

23. Journal of Charles Napier, August 12, 1813, in William F. P. Napier, *The Life and Opinions of General Sir Charles James Napier*, 4 vols. (London, 1857), 1:221.

24. London *Morning Chronicle*, July 9, 1813.

25. Quoted in Edgar S. Maclay, *A History of American Privateers* (New York, 1899), 275.

26. *Niles' Register*, 4 (May 15, 1813), 182; 5 (January 8, 1814), 312; and 6 (June 25, 1814), 279.

27. Quoted in Scott, *Memoirs*, 1:129. Where Scott got this quote is unknown, and although the words are now part U.S. Army lore, Riall may never have uttered them.

28. Letter of James Miller, July 28, 1814, in Ernest A. Cruikshank, ed., *The Documentary History of the Campaign on the Niagara Frontier*, 9 vols. (Welland, Ont., 1896–1908), 1:105.

29. Gaines to secretary of war, August 23, 1814, in U.S. Department of War, *Letters Received ... Registered Series*, microfilm series M221 reel 61.

30. Robertson to Daniel Pring, September 12, 1814, in William Wood, ed., *Select British Documents of the Canadian War of 1812,* 3 vols. (Toronto, 1920–28), 3:374.

31. London *Morning Chronicle,* November 18, 1814.

32. Quoted in Henry Adams, *History of the United States of America during the Administrations of Jefferson and Madison,* rev. ed. (with corrections), edited by Earl N. Harbert, 2 vols. (New York: Library of America, 1986), 2:998.

33. [George R. Gleig], *A Subaltern in America, Comprising His Narrative of the Campaigns of the British Army . . . during the Late War* (Philadelphia, 1833), 67.

34. William Thornton to the Public, August 30, 1814, in Washington *National Intelligencer,* September 7, 1814.

35. James Scott, *Recollections of a Naval Life,* 3 vols. (London, 1834), 3:314–15.

36. Edward Codrington to wife, September 10, 1814, in Lady Jane Bourchier, *Memoir of the Life of Admiral Sir Edward Codrington,* 2 vols. (London, 1873), 1:320.

37. *Naval Chronicle* 32 (July–December 1814), 244.

38. Speech of Alexander Baring, December 1, 1814, in T. C. Hansard, ed., *The Parliamentary Debates from the Year 1803 to the Present Time,* [First Series], 41 vols. (London, 1803–20), 29:651.

39. Proclamation of Thomas Boyle, [August 27, 1814], in *Niles' Register* 7 (January 7, 1815), 290–91.

40. Izard to secretary of war, July 31, 1814, in U.S. Department of War, *Letters Received . . . Registered Series,* microfilm series M221 reel 62.

41. Prevost to Earl Bathurst, August 27, 1814, in Cruikshank, *Niagara Frontier,* 1:180.

42. Alexander Contee Hanson to Robert Goodloe Harper, October 9, 1814, in Harper Papers, microfilm edition, reel 2, Maryland Historical Society, Baltimore.

43. Speech of Richard Stockton, December 10, 1814, in *AC,* 13-3, 849.

44. G. C. Moore Smith, ed., *The Autobiography of Lieutenant-General Sir Harry Smith,* 2 vols. (London, 1902), 1:247.

45. Madison to Congress, March 4, 1813, in *AC,* 12-2, 123.

46. George McFeeley to Alexander Smyth, [November 1812], in Cruikshank, *Niagara Frontier,* 4:234

Index

peace, 1, 50, 89, 130, 133. *See also individual Indians, tribes, and battles*

Insurance rates, marine, 42, 69, 111

"Ironsides." *See Constitution,* USS

Iroquois Indians, U.S., 84; British (Grand River), 5, 35

Italy, 12

Izard, George, 89, 93, 118

Jackson, Andrew, vii, 3, 65–68, 122–26, 136, 141

Java, HMS, 39

Jefferson, Thomas, 25

Johnson, Richard M., 50–51

Jones, William, 3

Kentucky, 21, 63

Kentucky rifle, 16, 143

Key, Francis Scott, 108–9

Kickapoo Indians, 23

Kingston (ON), 51, 53, 90–91

Lacolle Mill (QC), Battle of, 36

Lake Borgne, Battle of, 123

Lake Champlain, 3–4, 26, 35–36, 61; Battle of, 94–96, 112, 135

Lake Erie, 3–4, 36, 59, 80–83; Battle of, 3–4, 47–51, 75, 95, 135

Lake Huron, 27, 80–82, 136

Lake Michigan, 27

Lake Ontario, 3–4, 36, 50–54, 59, 78, 85, 90–91

Lake St. Clair, 80

Lambert, Henry, 39

Lawrence, James, 74–75

Lawrence, USS, 47, 75

Lawrence, William, 127

Lee, "Light–Horse" Harry, 13

Lee, Robert E., 13

Leipzig (Germany), Battle of, 79

Leonard, Nathan, 58

Leopard, HMS, 8

Levant, HMS, 128

Lewis, Morgan, 55

Lewiston (NY), 55

Library of Congress, 104

Licenses, British, 69

Little Belt affair, 9

Liverpool, Lord, 3–4

Liverpool Packet, British privateer, 42

Loans, U.S., 115–17, 119–20, 175

Logistics. *See* Supply lines; Supply service

Loyalists (British), 24, 36

Lundy's Lane (ON), Battle of, 84–88, 135

Lyon's Creek (ON), Battle of, 89

Macdonough, Thomas, 3, 94–96, 141

Macedonian, HMS and USS, 38, 143

Machias (ME), 101

Mackinac Island (MI), 27, 30, 50, 80–82, 136

Macomb, Alexander, 93–94

Madison, Dolley, 104, 139

Madison, James, 1–2, 11, 37, 103, 120; and deserters, 114; and election of 1812, 43; and peace negotiations, 128–32; as war leader, 139–40

Maine, 96, 100–101, 112, 118, 130–31

Malacca, Strait of, 127

Malcolm's Mills (ON), Battle of, 83

Manchester (NY), 58

Marines: British, 71, 91–92, 110; British Colonial, 138; U.S., 72, 103

Martial law, 125–26

Maryland, 13, 71

Massachusetts, 21, 96, 100, 102, 121–22

Maumee River, 32, 45

McArthur, Duncan, 83

McClure, George, 57–58

McDouall, Robert, 81

McFeely, George, 139

Medical treatment, 20–21

Melville Island (NS), 21

Mexican War, 11, 145

Miami Indians, 30–31

Militia, British, 133

Militia, Canadian, 15, 37

Militia, U.S., 14–16, 21, 57, 64–66, 71; and conscription, 119; and New England, 120; refusal of to serve outside country, 34, 36, 61

Miller, James, 86–88

Minnesota, 130

Mississinewa (IN), Battle of, 31–32

Mississippi River, 124, 126, 130

Mitchell, George B., 91

Mobile (AL), 65, 126–27

Mobile Bay, 123
Mohawk Indians, 5, 35, 62
Mohawk River, 91
Monroe (MI), 32
Monroe, James, 3, 11, 103, 120, 141
Montreal (QC), 24–26, 44, 57, 60–62, 78, 93, 114, 136
Moose Island (ME), 100–101
Moraviantown (ON), Battle of, 49
Morris, Charles, 101
Morrison, Joseph W., 62
Murray, John, 58
Muskets, 15–16

Nancy, HMS, 82
Nantucket (MA), 99, 111
Napoleon, vii, 79, 141
Napoleonic Wars, vii, 4–6, 15, 26, 79, 111, 124, 135, 140, 144
National Bank, U.S., 116–17, 119
National debt, U.S., 115–16, 136–37. *See also* Loans, U.S.; Bonds, U.S.
Nautilus, East India Company cruiser, 132
Navy, Royal (British), 13, 21; and blockades, 69–71, 96–99; and campaign of 1812, 37–42; and campaign of 1813, 71–76, 136; and campaign of 1814, 96–110; and campaign of 1815, 127–28; and *Chesapeake* affair, 8–9; and impressment, 5, 7; and ship seizures, 7. *See also* Lake Borgne, Battle of; Champlain, Battle of; Lake Erie, Battle of; Lake Ontario
Navy, U.S., 18–19, 115, 141; and campaign of 1812, 37–41, 135; and campaign of 1813, 73–76; and campaign of 1814, 111–12; and campaign of 1815, 127–28. *See also* Lake Borgne, Battle of; Lake Champlain, Battle of; Lake Erie, Battle of; Lake Ontario
New Brunswick (Canada), 24, 42, 100
New England, 11–13, 69, 96–97, 100, 113, 117–22, 137
New Hampshire, 121
New Orleans (LA), Battle of, vii, 14, 122–26, 136, 138, 141
New Orleans, USS, 90
New York (NY), 18, 57, 70–71, 75, 127
New York (state), 35, 69; and British inva-

sion of 1813, 57–59; and British invasion of 1814, 80, 93–96, 112, 135
Niagara-on-the-Lake (ON), 57
Newark (ON), 57, 59
Newfoundland (Canada), 24
Niagara, USS, 47, 49
Niagara Falls, 85–86
Niagara front, 4; and campaign of 1812, 33–37, 136; and campaign of 1813, 54–59, 77–78, 136; and campaign of 1814, 80, 83–90, 93, 112, 135
Niagara Peninsula (ON), 54, 85
Niagara River, 3, 5, 26, 44, 55, 80, 84
Night Engagement (LA), 123
Non-exportation law, U.S., 9
Non-importation law, U.S., 9
Norfolk (VA), 72–73
Norristown (PA), 12
North Point (MD), Battle of, 107, 135
North West Company, 27, 81
Northwest, U.S. *See* Old Northwest
Norton, John, 5, 35
Nottawasaga (ON), Battle of, 82
Nottawasaga River, 82

Oaths, 101
Ohio, 27, 31–32, 45–47
Ohio, USS, 87
"Old Hickory." *See* Jackson, Andrew
"Old Ironsides." *See Constitution,* USS
Old Northwest, 3, 22–23; and campaign of 1812, 27–33, 63; and campaign of 1813, 44–50, 77, 135; and campaign of 1814, 80–83; and peace negotiations, 130, 145
Oneida Indians, 92
Orders-in-Council, British, 5, 7, 128
Oswego (NY), 91–92; Battle of, 91
Oswego Falls (NY), 91
Oswego River, 91
Overton, Walter H., 126

Pakenham, Edward, 4, 123–24
Paris, Treaty of (1783), 100
Parker, Peter, 110
Passamaquoddy Bay, 100
Patapsco River, 108
Pax Americana, 146
Pax Britannia, 146